The Annotated Secession Papers

Authors

Barry Lee Clark, Brian McCandliss, Michael Peirce, Dr. Walter E. Block, Dr. Thomas E. Woods Jr., Dr. Kevin L. Clauson, Kirkpatrick Sale, Dr. Forrest McDonald, Gene H. Kizer, Jr., Dr. Thomas J. Dilorenzo, Dr. Donald W. Livingston

Editor
Barry Lee Clark

ISBN-13: 978-1983255045

Publication Date

February 20, 2016, First Edition
June 21, 2018, Second Edition

Publisher

The Calhoun Institute, Abbeville, SC
www.calhouninstitute.com

Purpose, Use and Copyright

In the mid to late 2000's the authors of the works contained within this publication gave permission to include their essays as part of The American Secessionist's Project to develop a collection of modern thoughts on the concept of secession. Nothing contained herein should be construed to deprive the original author of the rights to their work.   This publication was developed under the understanding that the author(s) provided permission for inclusion of their work in the original papers. Finally, I have edited each original work to include additional footnotes that may expand and further illuminate the points made.

This publication is presented within the public domain for use as an educational tool and for additional commentary with the explicit expectation that the authors of all essays contained herein will receive just recognition for their work and ideas and that the combined work is represented as such.

*Dr. Forrest McDonald passed away before permission was secured for his piece, it has been previously posted under the Fair Use Doctrine and is included herein.

The second edition to this work represents both a cleaning up of formatting and other errors from the first addition and an expansion of ideas based upon events, thoughts and occurrences over the seventeen years than have passed since some of the earliest article were written.

All citations added in the second edition follow the APA in-line style for ease of digital reading (with the but a few exceptions). The MLA citations from the first addition have been left intact with only changes in the format for compliance with digital publishing standards.

Published by **The Calhoun Institute**, 2016 First Edition, 2018 Second Edition

Table of Contents

Introduction

Since the original release of the first edition of The
Annotated Secessionist Papers, the world has not ceased
to view secession and devolution as a legitimate
recourse for people across the globe that seek more
responsive democratic representation. Scottish
independence nearly became a reality. BREXIT did occur,
there have been quasi-serious discussions of CALEXIT
and there is currently a ballot proposition to devolve
California into three separate states. In Europe, there
are currently twenty-one active and real secession or
devolution movements. [1] The concept, tried twice on
the American continent and threaten on one other
occasion, was not debunked in 1861-1865. It remains a
viable alternative to governments that have grown too
large to effectively represent diverse interests. Secession
and devolution must remain relevant in political
conversations and solutions.

The intent of this work remains the same, to keep the
topic of secession in the domain of public and academic
discourse as a valid and viable political alternative to an
increasingly diverse and divided world that daily become
less governable by large, central governments.

Introduction to First Edition

The idea has become a very "anti-American" concept according to the mainstream. It is conceivable that wrapped up in the ongoing fervor surrounding terrorism and the continual expansion and evolution of what is defined as a terrorist combined with a central government that each year amasses greater authority over the citizenry and the very definition of words and concepts that a time may soon come when even talking about States' Rights or secession may be termed terroristic and dangerous. The most dangerous thing that could happen to a people and a society is that of acquiring an inability to talk honestly about issues past and present. It is with the goal of ensuring that an honest discussion of secession continues, even if on the margins of mainstream thought and discussion.

Several of the authors wrote of secession in the papers presented herein with an eye toward presenting secession as a viable option to contemporary problems of government and truly representative democracy within the confines of a republican form of governance. From a purely practical standpoint, this is obviously problematic. Detractors point to the bloody outcome of the first attempt in the American continent and state the issue is settled, the central government simply would not allow it. Those that may acknowledge the legitimacy of the concept often declare that practical implementation is impossible for a variety of reasons discussed throughout the commentaries that accompany each essay. In the end, secession is essentially taken to be either illegitimate or impractical and has been relegated to the fringe of political theory discussion. One additional argument that generally stops discussion of secession or builds a strawman out of those that discuss it favorably is the idea that it is tied up with the requirement for war and bloodshed. The entire Soviet Union devolved into separate nation-states without war, Quebec and Scotland have each voted to secede in recent years and if those votes had been in the affirmative there would have been no bloodshed. One could argue that every major election in a democracy has the potential to turn into violence, and in some nations, this is often the case, it is not an expected occurrence in Western democracies.

Those that discuss secession as a potential solution to current political problems do not advocate violence or war. Those that desire an honest discussion of the history and the historical, constitutional and legal theories surrounding the subject exist on the margins simply because the majority are content with accepting only one slanted version of the truth.

Why is it important to talk about secession? Few
people that believe secession is a legitimate political
theory, right and recourse also believe that in a practical
sense it is achievable, reasonable or even preferable.
Devolution is a complicated matter and requires a more
or less united political will among a people within a
region or area – within the confines of modern America,
it seems unlikely any such will of a sufficient majority
will soon emerge, anywhere. The question thus remains,
why even discuss the subject?

It is important to honestly discuss the matter because
it goes to the very heart of how the Union of States was
formed, what the Constitution was to mean and what
relation the central government was to have to the
people. Many of our contemporary political problems
stem directly from a failure to understand foundational
principles. Perhaps in engendering more honest
discussions about foundational principles we might
actually see contemporary problems more correctly.

The purpose of this work is therefore three-fold.   First,
there should exist, and should continue to exist, an
honest discussion related to the principles behind the
reason secession was considered legitimate before 1865.
Second, we must continue to discuss the history,
interpretation, and implementation of our laws. Third, if
we are to forever remain a free people, we must
reacquaint ourselves with all of the options available to a
free people.

About the Authors

*denotes authors that for various reasons penned under a pseudonym.

Barry Lee Clark, editor and contributor to *The Annotated Secessionist Papers*. **www.barryclark.info**

*EL Cid** Barry Clark's pen name in the 2000s

Brian McCandliss - is a business and economics graduate of Liberty University in Lynchburg, VA, a law student, and a businessman in Detroit, Michigan.

Michael Peirce

Dr. Walter E. Block - is a professor of economics at Loyola University New Orleans and holds the Harold E. Wirth Eminent Scholar Endowed Chair and Professor of Economics. **www.walterblock.com**

*Hugh Williamson**- is Professor of Political Science and the author of a book about Calhoun.

Dr. Thomas E. Woods Jr. - A 1994 graduate of Harvard College, holds a Ph.D. in history from Columbia University and is currently a professor of history at Suffolk Community College in Brentwood, New York. He is also the author of the recent book The Politically Incorrect Guide to American History. **www.tomwoods.com**.

Kevin L. Clauson - B.A. (International Relations), B.S. (Chemistry), M.A. (Political Science), Marshall University; J.D. (Law), West Virginia University. President, Christ College; President, The Patrick Henry Institute; Former Chair, Government Department, Liberty University; Professor of Government, Helms School of Government, Liberty University; Former Assistant Professor of Political Science, Grove City College. Married (since 1982); four children.

Kirkpatrick Sale - director of The Middlebury Institute and the author of Human Scale as well as numerous other works.

Dr. Forrest McDonald -An award-winning internationally known historian taught at The University of Alabama from 1976 until he retired in 2002 as Distinguished University Research Professor. He authored twenty books and over one hundred articles. **http://history.ua.edu/faculty/forrest-mcdonald/**

Gene H. Kizer, Jr. - Graduated magna cum laude from the College of Charleston (SC) in 2000 at middle age with History Departmental Honors, the Rebecca Motte American History Award, and the highest award for the History Department, the Outstanding Student Award. In addition to his latest book, Slavery Was Not the Cause of the War Between the States, The Irrefutable Argument., he is the author of The Elements of Academic Success, How to Graduate Magna Cum Laude from College (or how to just graduate, PERIOD!), a 364-page softcover book, and Charleston, SC Short Stories, Book One, an eBook on Amazon. He lives on James Island in Charleston where he is also broker-in-charge of Charleston Saltwater Realty. **http://www.bonniebluepublishing.com/**

Thomas J. Dilorenzo -is the author of The Real Lincoln: A New Look at Abraham Lincoln, His Agenda, and an Unnecessary War, (Three Rivers Press/Random House). His latest book is How Capitalism Saved America: The Untold Story of Our Country's History, from the Pilgrims to the Present (Crown Forum/Random House, August 2004).

Dr. Donald W. Livingston - is a former Professor of Philosophy at Emory University with an expertise in the writings of David Hume. In 2003 he founded the Abbeville Institute, which is devoted to the study of Southern culture and political ideas. He is an author and contributor to numerous books and papers and has been called "the godfather of the modern secessionist movement".

First Things

By **Barry Lee Clark**

Secession in the United States is a much maligned and misunderstood right. However, Ignorance and hatred of the concept in no way diminish its status as a right. Our very Declaration of Independence is a secessionist document.

We hold these truths to be self-evident, that all men are created equal; that they are endowed by their Creator with certain unalienable rights; and that among these, are life, liberty, and the pursuit of happiness. That to secure these rights, governments are instituted among men, deriving their just powers from the consent of the governed; that whenever any form of government becomes destructive of these ends, it is the right of the people to alter or to abolish it, and to institute a new government, laying its foundation on such principles, and organizing its powers in such form, to affect their safety and happiness.

Abraham Lincoln himself was a defender of secession at one point in his career:

"Any people anywhere being inclined and having the power have the right to rise up and shake off the existing government and form a new one which suits them better. This is a most valuable, a most sacred right-a right which we hope and believe is to liberate the world. Nor is this right confined to cases in which the whole people of an existing government may choose to exercise it. Any portion of such people that may revolutionize and make their own so much of the territory as they inhabit."

This excerpt is taken from Lincoln's "If You Can Secede You May" (Mexico) speech.[2]

The right of secession in the US goes to the very heart of how and who formed the United States. John C. Calhoun in his work Discourse on The Constitution and Government of the United States lays out the argument that: [3]

1) the United States is a federal, not national government. It is a government representing a collective of states, each of which retains its own sovereignty.
2) The People established their respective states; the states established the federal government.
3) The United States government and the various states have a contractual arrangement (a compact to use Calhoun's word), when either violates the contract it can be nullified or terminated

A Brief Primer on the Origin, Nature and Role of the Federal Compact

It is pointless to discuss the justness of the principle of secession without first discussing our federal compact. Our thoughts on the perpetuity of the Federal Union have been continually reinforced since 1892 by items like the Pledge of Allegiance with the "indivisible" phrase (never mind that the Pledge itself was written by a socialist with grand ideas of a Social Utopian in the US based upon very un-American ideals). US history as taught in most US schools only adds to the confusion and misunderstanding concerning the true nature of the federal compact as envisioned by those that created the nation.

The framers of the Constitution were very careful to establish limits and checks on the central government. Many today read the Constitution of the United States and see rights and powers delegated to the States and the people. The framers of the Constitution saw the document as rather as a dispensation of very specific and limited powers to the central government; all other rights, powers and liberties not specifically given to the central government were to remain with the States or the people.

Wherefore does the Government of the United States gain legitimacy to govern? Was the federal government born of popular affirmation? Did it gain sovereignty from the King of England via the terms of peace granting the thirteen colonies independence? In fact, the central government was born of and created by the independent thirteen colonies. King George III granted independence to the several colonies as free and independent states. The British did not deal with or recognize the central government.

The question of which political entities had sovereignty and independence first is clear. The can be no legitimate debate on this point.

In forming the central government, the states did not relinquish or surrender their inherent sovereignty. Like all associations of sovereign entities since the dawn of time, the communal association of free and sovereign states in 1789 was akin to the formation of a club. Its members chartered the club, a set of rules and guidelines was established, and certain rights were delegated to the club in order for it to function. The acts of forming and joining the club in no way diminished the status of the members.

The term "delegated" is key in this assessment of the relationship between the central government and the states. It is impossible for an inferior entity to delegate powers to a superior. In such a case the proper term would be "surrender". Delegation occurs between a superior to a subordinate or between equals. The words used in the formation of the Union were those of delegation to the central government from the states; not of surrendering of powers. It is apparent that the strongest position intended for the Federal government to hold in relation to the States was that of an equal.

The words used in the Virginia Act of Ratification of the United States Constitution state these points well:

"We, the delegates of the People of Virginia, duly elected in behalf of the people of Virginia, declare and make known, that the powers granted under the Constitution, being derived from the people of the United States, may be resumed by them, whensoever the same shall be perverted to their injury or oppression; and that every power not granted thereby with them and at their will: that, therefore, no right, of any denomination, can be canceled, abridged, restrained, or modified."

It is clear that Virginia as the sovereign agent of the People of Virginia neither surrendered rights or sovereignty in the ratification of the Constitution. Furthermore, at ratification, they made it clear that the agreement would survive only contingent upon the continued benefit to the people.

Who and What Came First?

The question, were the States sovereign nations, is addressed in throughout this work. This is an important question because it speaks directly to what political entities gave rise to the Federal government. Our history is replete with examples of the sovereignty of the States before, during and after the compact that gave birth to the United States, a point proven several times over in the chapters that follow.

Accepting that the States were independent and sovereign long before the creation of the Union of States begs the question: who makes the rules, the parent or the child? Assume for a moment that in thirty years one of the nations of Europe desires to withdraw from the European Union. Would we as Americans believe that a body created by independent and sovereign States should morally or ethically force this nation and people to remain against their will?

What then of the Federal Compact?

The Articles of Confederation that gave rise to the first voluntary Union of the various free and independent American states was written to be perpetual. Such words are clearly used in that document, however "perpetual" in this case was short-lived.

The Articles themselves were clear on the matter of state sovereignty at the time of what most Americans consider the birth of the United States. Article II states:

Each state retains its sovereignty, freedom, independence, and every power, jurisdiction, and right, which is not by this Confederation expressly delegated to the United States in Congress assembled.[4]

The concept that Men can form perfect Unions that in perpetuity might serve the needs of all of mankind so burdened to find their lot that of Citizen is both preposterous and contrary to the historical fact. Clearly, the first "perpetual" union was imperfect, and as shall be demonstrated on the pages that follow, the creation of the Constitutional Union that followed was nothing more than nine of the original thirteen states seceding.

The Undeniable Legality of Secession

At the most fundamental and basic level of our political belief system as Americans rests the idea that men ought to be free to determine their own form of government. Our Declaration of Independence states this fact clearly:

...That to secure these rights, Governments are instituted among Men, deriving their just powers from the consent of the governed, --That whenever any Form of Government becomes destructive of these ends, it is the Right of the People to alter or to abolish it, and to institute new Government, laying its foundation on such principles and organizing its powers in such form, as to them shall seem most likely to effect their Safety and Happiness...

Few Americans would deny that our founders in 1776 had among other inalienable rights the justification and right to assert a form of government "most likely to effect Safety and Happiness". With such a strong sense of the rights of the people inherent in our most foundational of beliefs, it is amazing that Americans so easily view these concepts as applicable only to another time and place.

Secession is legal under natural law, biblical law and in accordance with the State/Federal compact theory of government.

The Unconstitutionality of Using Force to Coerce a State

President James Buchanan stated succinctly in a speech before Congress, December 1860 that the Constitution does not delegate to the Federal government the power to use force against a state:

"The question fairly stated is, Has the Constitution delegated to Congress the power to coerce a State into submission which is attempting to withdraw or has actually withdrawn from the Confederacy? If answered in the affirmative, it must be on the principle that the power has been conferred upon Congress to declare and to make war against a State. After much serious reflection, I have arrived at the conclusion that no such power has been delegated to Congress or to any other department of the Federal Government. It is manifest upon an inspection of the Constitution that this is not among the specific and enumerated powers granted to Congress, and it is equally apparent that its exercise is not 'necessary and proper for carrying into execution' any one of these powers. So far from this power having been delegated to Congress, it was expressly refused by the Convention which framed the Constitution.

It appears from the proceedings of that body that on the 31st May, 1787, the clause ' authorizing an exertion of the force of the whole against a delinquent State" came up for consideration. Mr. Madison opposed it in a brief but powerful speech, from which I shall extract but a single sentence. He observed:

'The use of force against a State would look more like a declaration of war than an infliction of punishment, and would probably be considered by the party attacked as a dissolution of all previous compacts by which it might be bound. Upon his motion, the clause was unanimously postponed, and was never, I believe, again presented. Soon afterwards, on the 8th June, 1787, when incidentally adverting to the subject, he said: "Any government for the United States formed on the supposed practicability of using force against the unconstitutional proceedings of the States would prove as visionary and fallacious as the government of Congress," evidently meaning the then existing Congress of the old Confederation.

Without descending to particulars, it may be safely asserted that the power to make war against a State is at variance with the whole spirit and intent of the Constitution. Suppose such a war should result in the conquest of a State; how are we to govern it afterwards? Shall we hold it as a province and govern it by despotic power? In the nature of things, we could not by physical force control the will of the people and compel them to elect Senators and Representatives to Congress and to perform all the other duties depending upon their own volition and required from the free citizens of a free State as a constituent member of the Confederacy. But if we possessed this power, would it be wise to exercise it under existing circumstances? The object would doubtless be to preserve the Union. War would not only present the most effectual means of destroying it, but would vanish all hope of its peaceable reconstruction.

Besides, in the fraternal conflict a vast amount of blood and treasure would be expended, rendering future reconciliation between the States impossible. In the meantime, who can foretell what would be the sufferings and privations of the people during its existence? The fact is that our Union rests upon public opinion, and can never be cemented by the blood of its citizens shed in civil war. If it cannot live in the affections of the people, it must one day perish. Congress possesses many means of preserving it by conciliation, but the sword was not placed in their hand to preserve it by force." [5]

A strict and reasoned interpretation of the Constitution supports Buchanan's point of view. As discussed previously the majority of the US Constitution up to and including the first ten amendments deals with powers delegated to the Federal Government and rights reserved to the People and the States. It is inconceivable that such a document was framed and a compact entered into that would deny rights and freedom to the people. It is inconceivable that a free state would voluntarily enter into an agreement with another party that authorized force to be used against the smaller member in the event of a disagreement.

The States as free and independent entities, having just won their independence from Britain, certainly did not endow the Federal government with the right to use force to coerce a state. Neither did the Union by mere fact of its existence inherit the right from some unseen and unwritten rule or code of law. The use of force to coerce a state is comparable to one nation invading another to establish their will. Our Western tradition dismisses this form of diplomacy as do all modern codes of relations among states. The invasion and coercion of one people by another is wrong in every instance that history has recorded it. The principles of *Jus Ad Bellum* that have more or less guided Western relations for centuries forbid this sort of behavior.

The entire notion of forcing another state or nation to abide by the rules of another ought to be as offensive to the American mind as Hitler's war on Europe in 1941.

Theories of Secession [6]

In order to scope the arguments that will follow it is necessary to highlight some of the political theories that justify secession in general.

Primary Right of Secession

Holds that a group has a basic right to secede regardless of whether injustices have been committed or not. This is also called unilateral right secession.

Nationalist Variant of Primary Right

Holds that every nation (territorially contiguous ethnic/cultural group) has the right to establish its own state (country) if they choose and may do so unilaterally and without any other justification.

Liberal Primary Right

Holds that because government's legitimacy derives solely from consent, any group of people may withdraw their territory from an existing state and set up a new state, so long as a majority of the group agrees and the rights of the minority are respected in the new state.

Remedial Right Only

Holds that a national group enjoys a unilateral right to secede if and only if its members have suffered serious, fundamental injustices and secession is the only alternative left to remedy those injustices. RRO theories strictly confine the right to secede to a small set of cases.

Partial Right Variant of Remedial Right

An expansion of the former with conditions. Anthony Birch, in "Another Liberal Theory of Secession", states that one of the following prior conditions must be present for secession to be justified:

1.The seceding region was included in the state by force and its people have displayed a continuing refusal to give full consent to the union;

2.The national government has failed in a serious way to protect the basic rights and security of the citizens of the region;
3.The democratic system has failed to safeguard the legitimate political and economic interests of the region, either because the representative process is biased against the region or because the executive authorities contrive to ignore the results of that process;

or

4.The national government has ignored or rejected an explicit or implicit bargain between sections that was entered into as a way of preserving the essential interests of a section that might find itself outvoted by a national majority.

State-Federal Contract Theory

Holds that in the United States a contract (compact) exists between the federal government and the various states. This theory is best articulated by John C. Calhoun (although Calhoun did used the term compact rather than contract) and was the bedrock behind the states of the former Confederacy declaring their independence.   This theory is easily combined in application with the above theories in various circumstances.

Secessionist No. 1: Why Secession

By El Cid
2004

Not since the crisis of 1861 has a moment more clearly presented itself for the heirs to the birthright of the Republic formed in 1789 to reassert the principles of our founding. The various liberties and inalienable rights enjoyed by the people as a natural result of God's gift to man and the sovereignty of the several States has been gradually eroded over the course of the history of this nation. Those that have stood on the principles of States Rights and individual liberty have always suffered the disadvantage of lacking the moral high ground in their cause. It was thus in the 1860; and it was so in the 1960's. Without the power of legitimate moral issues and principles efforts to assert the Sovereignty of the States has failed. These failures have created a set of precedence that has allowed the power of the central government to usurp the State on more trivial and mundane matters. The sum and total result is a current federal government that lives and operates far outside of the bound envisioned by our founders. To the State this means a loss of sovereignty and freedom of action. To the individual this means tyranny imposed by a government that is far removed geographically and indifferent to the needs, values and principles of the individual.

As citizens we find now that we have a choice. We might submit to the lot that we have inherited via generations of central government usurpation and apathy of the populace. To accept and embrace this option is to acquiesce to of life and a future in which the federal government determines what is moral, what is right and what principle we and our children shall live under. On the surface the benefits of living under a socialist system of strong central control might seem palatable to many. The perks of the current system of welfare, managed healthcare, and governmental regulation of nearly every aspect of life appeal to a certain class of people. These are individuals have determined to surrender their birthright of freedom for a paternalistic system that provides for them what they ought to provide for themselves.

Here a series of papers will be presented that discuss the various aspects of this plan; the merits of following and supporting such an action; counter-arguments to the naysayers and stone throwers; and encouragements to those that believe that government is best that governs least.

Recedite, plebes! Gero rem imperialem
El Cid

Secessionist No. 2: The Right to Govern

By El Cid
June 01, 2004

Since the dawn of history man has formed associations for mutual benefit and protection. H.G Wells provides an excellent overview of the trends and tendencies of collectivism that carried mankind from tribal existence to the Age of Imperialism, even if he was ultimately wrong in many of his interpretations.

His volume entitled *The Outline of History* written in 1920 was an attempt to answer the questions of how man moved from relatively diverse and independent associations to imperial nation-states that waged war on a global scale. Wells' work is unique and significant in its treatment of history. Any thinking man that sincerely wishes to understand the nature and purpose of government ought to be familiar with Wells' outline, if not his conclusions. [7]

We accept readily the necessity for government. The reality of the world we live in is such that without government to restrain the evil around us the individual would be faced with a daily fight for survival. The acceptance of common association in the form of government necessitates that the individual delegate some rights and to the government. In this sense government is a necessary evil.

Free men have always understood the inherent evil nature of government.

Governments weld tremendous power over those whom they rule. Invariably all systems of government that are restrained in power solely by the government itself move from liberty to tyranny. Historically this has always been so. When those that control the government establish that the government is superior to the creators and act as the sole judge of the propriety of expanding governmental power tyranny has already begun to take hold.

"Government is not reason; it is not eloquence; it is force! Like fire, it is a dangerous servant and a fearful master!" A quote often misapplied to George Washington describe government adequately.

What then is good government? John C. Calhoun stated in *Disposition on Government* that:

"The infinite Being, Creator of all, has assigned to man the social and political state, as best not only to impel him into the social state, but to make government necessary for man's preservation and well-being."[8]

This is a principle shared by those that founded America as well as the majority of the thinkers and philosophers of the century preceding our founding. Our own Declaration of Independence speaks of the freedom granted to man by God to establish government. Good government is that which governs least and abides by the documents and agreements that gave it birth. Plato in The Republic acknowledged that his ideal version of representative government must be based upon the principle of a God that underpinned the legitimacy of government itself. [9]

The framers of the Constitution were very careful to establish limits and checks on the central government. Many read the Constitution of the United States today and see rights and powers delegated to the States and the people. The framers of the Constitution saw the document as rather as a dispensation of very specific and limited powers to the central government; all other rights, powers and liberties not specifically given to the central government were to remain with the States or the people. [10]

Wherefore does the Government of the United States gain legitimacy to govern? Was the federal government born of popular affirmation? Did it gain sovereignty from the King of England via the terms of peace granting the thirteen colonies independence? In fact, the central government was born of and created by the independent thirteen colonies. King George III granted independence to the several colonies as free and independent states. [11]

The question of which political entities had sovereignty and independence first is clear. The can be no legitimate debate on this point.

In forming the central government, the states did not relinquish or surrender their inherent sovereignty. Like all associations of sovereign entities since the dawn of time the communal association of free and sovereign states in 1789 was akin to the formation of a club. Its members chartered the club, a set of rules and guidelines was established, and certain rights were delegated to the club in order for it to function. The acts of forming and joining the club in no way diminished the status of the members.

The term "delegated" is key in this assessment of the relationship between the central government and the states. It is impossible for an inferior entity to delegate powers to a superior. In such a case the proper term would be "surrender". Delegation occurs between a superior to a subordinate or between equals. The words used in the formation of the Union were those of delegation to the central government from the states; not of surrender of powers. It is apparent that the strongest position intended for the Federal government to hold in relation to the States was that of an equal, the weakest that of the child to the parent.

The words used in the Virginia Act of Ratification of the United States Constitution state these points well: [12]

"We, the delegates of the People of Virginia, duly elected….in behalf of the people of Virginia, declare and make known, that the powers granted under the Constitution , being derived from the people of the United States, may be resumed by them, whensoever the same shall be perverted to their injury or oppression; and that every power not granted thereby with them and at their will: that, therefore, no right , of any denomination, can be canceled, abridged, restrained, or modified."

It is clear that Virginia as the sovereign agent of the People of Virginia neither surrendered rights or sovereignty in the ratification of the Constitution. Furthermore, at ratification they made it clear that the agreement would survive only contingent upon the continued benefit to the people. [13]

The central government rules by the consent of the sovereign states that gave it birth. Those states gain their sovereignty from their citizens; the people. The right of the Federal government to rule is based on nothing more complicated than that. So long as the government rules by the consent of the people it is moral and legitimate. Whenever the government ceases to abide by the compact that gave it birth or usurps powers not delegated to it there will exist illegitimacy.

Recedite, plebes! Gero rem imperialem
El Cid

Secessionist No. 3: A Brief Early History of

By El Cid

To the people of the various united states:

Many have and will falsely claim that secession is a concept alien to the republican and democratic concepts and principles of our American heritage. This is an assertion that rest far outside of reality and is dishonest to the historical fact. The idea of any form of government existing perpetually without the hope of mechanism for change is borne of an ideology that is itself foreign and alien to freedom and liberty. Those that advocate such a notion are often the unwitting agents of tyranny and oppression. It is the idea that a government once created gains legitimacy and sovereignty greater than those that created it that makes subjects of men that were once citizens and slaves of a free people.

Our American history is filled with secession and movements toward political autonomy. Most Americans understand and celebrate many of the aspects of this fact. We understand that the early colonist to this land came seeking economic, religious and political freedom. Their desire to remove themselves from the clutches of a government that they felt did not represent their desires and values is something we look upon with admiration. So too do we celebrate the actions of the Thirteen Colonies in their efforts to declare themselves free and independent states. While most Americans understand that these were each movements to leave one form of government and establish another, the connection between those concepts and secession is lost on most modern Americans.

What then of the concept of perpetual Union on the American continent? What of the "perpetual union" of United Colonies of New England" formed in 1643? [14] This union that claimed to be "firm and perpetual" formed of "free and independent sovereignties" was dissolved in 1686. What of the withdrawal of nine states from the "perpetual union" of the Articles of Confederation in 1787? [15] What of the movement in 1814 of several New England states to withdraw from the federal union? [16]

American history is often taught in such a way that the American Revolution is viewed in terms of what the Continental Congress did. The idea that the war was an American war fought by a central government supports the idea of the central government having primacy in the American experience. The reality is that the war was much more democratic than republican and sectionalist rather than centrist. The majority of key victories won were accomplished by local troops and the efforts individual colonies. The Continental Congress was nothing more than an executive agent for exercising of the will of the colonies; and only when the colonies decided to allow such.

Significant is the fact that the treaty of peace signed by King George III granted independence to the Thirteen Colonies as free and independent states. These are facts that most Americans accept to one degree or another; even those that see the world through centrist blinders. [17]

Those that advocate the primacy of the central union will claim that sovereignty is indivisible and since the British crown had sole sovereignty over the American colonies that it was impossible for this sovereignty to then be subdivided among several colonies. The centrist would say that no matter the words used to grant independence to the American Colonies the intent must have been to grant sovereignty to one government. This premise is falsely placed based on the fact that the several colonies acted independently before and after independence, and the King clearly named the individual colonies and free and independent. The notion that British sovereignty was indivisible is falsely claimed by the fact that during the 17th Century sovereignty in the British Empire was indeed divided among the parliament and the monarch. We are all familiar with the refutation of the notion of the divine right of kings articulated so well by Milton and Locke. The anti-secessionist point of view that sovereignty could not have been divided is a throwback to this arcane notion of the primacy of kings and their right to rule.

A familiar claim of the federalist is that the Declaration of Independence was the founding document for the United States. This line of reasoning asserts that the various states gained their existence from the central government after independence. This is a hollow claim, unsupported by the ample evidence to the contrary.

Prior to the Declaration many of the colonies had deposed of their royal governors and installed instead men of their choosing. Most colonies had within their purview the right of colonial legislation. Years prior to the actual declaration of independence most of the thirteen colonies had a fair measure of self-rule. Virginia alone among the colonies declared her independence in May of 1776. The declaration in July of that year was merely a joint declaration of all the thirteen colonies. It was not the declaration of a unified nation.

Further examples of the independence and sovereignty of the colonies prior to independence include: During the Revolution New York and Vermont nearly declared war on each other. [18] This prompted Massachusetts in 1784 to declare her neutrality in the matter. Virginia declared herself bound by a treaty with France long before the Continental Congress decided to act on the treaty. These are acts of independent and sovereign nation-states. These events proceeded the signing of any compact giving birth to the United States.

The Articles of Confederation that gave rise to the first voluntary Union of the various free and independent American states was written to be perpetual. Such words are clearly used in that document. Centrist and anti-secessionist will point to that and claim that even in the late eighteenth-century Americans viewed the central government as indivisible. It is interesting to note that the Articles required a unanimous vote of all thirteen states to modify the terms of the agreement. The abandonment of the government created by the Articles and establishment of the government created by the Constitution was indeed an act of secession, it dissolved the old Union and created a new government. In the process several of the original states were left outside of the new government until they ratified the Constitution, in essence, again acting an independent and free states. This is of course a point not clearly covered in history classes and seldom understood by Americans.

The Articles themselves were clear on the matter of state sovereignty. Article II states:

"Each state retains its sovereignty, freedom, independence, and every power, jurisdiction, and right, which is not by this Confederation expressly delegated to the United States in Congress assembled." [19]

Key items from Article II to consider are the terms "delegated" and "united states in Congress assembled." Powers were delegated to the central government by the states; not surrendered. Furthermore, the United States in this usage refers to the states assembled by their representatives in congress. The idea that the United States held a position as a viable and separate entity was nebulous at this point. It is impossible to assert that the United States existed as a separate entity since 1776 when this article is read clearly and considering the other free and independent nation-state acts the States themselves undertook.

The Articles required a unanimous vote to modify the terms and conditions of the compact. In 1799, only nine of the thirteen states ratified the new constitution. [20] The nine that ratified the Constitution and began operating under a new form of government in fact seceded from the Confederation. The original Union was dissolved and a new association was created. For over a year there existed two forms of central government, one consisting of the states that had joined the Constitutional compact and one of states that remained loyal to the original Confederation, but in reality those states that had not ratified the Constitution functioned as independent nation-states. It is interesting to note that during this period ships entering New York harbor (New York being a state that had joined the Constitutional Union) from Rhode Island (a state that remained in the Confederation) were listed as Foreign vessels.

It is clear that the change from a central government under the Articles of Confederation to one under the Constitution was indeed a change of government; a bloodless revolution really. The Articles were clear in the method allowed for changing the terms; unanimous vote. The Articles also were clear in the expected perpetuity of the compact. Neither of these concepts held much validity when nine of the signatory states determined that it was in their best interest to abandon the agreement and form a new type of government. The very Constitution that the Unionist, centrist and anti-secessionist claim such holy veneration for was itself a product of secession and ignoring the rule of law.

Secession is indeed part and parcel of American heritage and our historical experience. Secession does not have to result in war. The ultimate decision as to whether war will result from an act of secession rest with those that wish to retain union and force others to remain in their club. This very notion of forcing others to do things against their will seems the most undemocratic idea of all.

Recedite, plebes! Gero rem imperialem
El Cid

Secessionist No. 4: Secession as the Ultimate Test of Democracy

By El Cid
2004

   America is a nation born of and endowed with a healthy and abiding sense of democratic principles. We have moved from a very republican form of government in which representatives elected by various means conducted the business of government to more recent arrangements in which our representatives are directly elected. Furthermore, the growing use of referendums of the body politic has come into general use to settle many matters. We believe in justice and in democracy.

   The fact that the concept of justice and democracy are not always compatible is a notion that we seldom ponder. In a system where 51% of the people are able to obtain what they want and 49% are consistently unable to influence the political process justice is an unobtainable goal. This assumes more than the loss of one particular election. I am speaking of a minority within the general population that holds values and principles at such variance with the majority that they may never hope to significantly influence political outcomes. When the difference in the values and principles of a segment of the population varies so greatly and minority groups are consistently left without an effective voice the will of the majority becomes tyranny for the minority.

   We acknowledge the right of all citizens to vote via the ballot box. Our system rewards those in the majority while denying representation for the minority. We do not so readily recognize the right of the people to vote with their feet. To simply decide that the political association is no longer in their best interest and therefore decide to leave that association.

Our own Declaration of Independence clearly states the true American view of "voting with one's feet":

"We hold these truths to be self-evident, that all men are created equal, that they are endowed by their Creator with certain unalienable Rights, that among these are Life, Liberty and the pursuit of Happiness. --That to secure these rights, Governments are instituted among Men, deriving their just powers from the consent of the governed, --That whenever any Form of Government becomes destructive of these ends, it is the Right of the People to alter or to abolish it, and to institute new Government, laying its foundation on such principles and organizing its powers in such form, as to them shall seem most likely to effect their Safety and Happiness." [21]

It seems that in the mind of those that advocate a strong, perpetual and indivisible union that the right of men to establish governments of and by their consent was a onetime event. To accept their argument one must accept that "times have changed". What we should ask what has really changed? Have principles changed? Principles are the very rocks upon which all is built. Principles never change. Men through selfishness and perversions attempt to change what principles mean but their attempts are always unsuccessful ultimately.

We would cry havoc if a club or religious organization denied its members the right to leave those organizations. If those entities attempted to restrain their members by force in order to keep them in their fold, we would promptly call upon the police to use force to free those that wished to leave. In America this seems to us to be justice and this is a concept we understand and support.

In contract law we are willing to see the letter and terms of an agreement carried out. However, when one party to the contract fails to live by the agreement we are perfectly willing to allow the aggrieved party relief from their portion of the contract. In our mind this is justice.

Why then is it such a difficult leap to apply these same principles to government and how we are each ruled? Are we property that belongs to the national government of our birth? Are we citizens of that government or subject to it? If a segment of the population believes that the contract with the government has been violated by the government itself who is the arbitrator of this dispute? Is the government itself the final judge of its own actions?

We are in fact not subjects to the central government. The people through the sovereignty that they granted to the states gave birth to the federal government. The people (the 14th Amendment notwithstanding) are citizens of the various states. It is the people through the sovereignty of their state that are the final judge of the federal government and the status of the contract of government. There is no other reasonable state of affairs. To accept the federal government as supreme to the entities that gave it birth and give it unilateral power to determine if its actions are just can only lead to tyranny.

In a nation that wishes to remain free the notion that the people retain the ultimate right to establish a form of government to their liking must remain paramount.

Recedite, plebes! Gero rem imperialem
El Cid

Secessionist No. 5: The Illegitimacy of the 14th Amendment

By El Cid

Some federalist and anti-secessionist will acquiesce to the logic and reasonableness of secession and independence movements in theory. They will tell you that the point is moot as it pertains to the nature of the United States government as that question was neatly answered not only by the failure of Southern forces to achieve independence in the 1860's but ultimately by the passage of the 14th Amendment.

The first point is frivolous. No matter of principle has ever been settled on the battlefield. Might does not make right. Might simply proves that might wins. It is the ugliest form or democratic expression; we have more so we get to have our way.

The 14th Amendment is a different case entirely. Taken at face value this amendment would seem to rob much of the steam from the idea of States' Rights. Specifically, section 1 of that amendment establishes United States citizens for the first time. Hitherto citizenship rested solely in the body of the states. The very act of stripping the states of their citizens and placing restrictions on the states as to their treatment of the new class of citizenry created under this act seem to remove from the people the power to express their will through the sovereignty of their state of citizenship.

The 14th Amendment changed the very face and nature of the Federal government. History lessons seldom term the enactment of this act as a transition from one form of government to another but that is exactly what occurred. The premise of the central government now having citizens in the various states and expanded power to manage and govern those citizens created a very different form of government. The enactment of the 14th Amendment was in fact the death of the old Constitutional Republic and the birth or a new form of government. No longer did states retain the authority for self-rule on items specifically reserved to them in the Constitution. No longer were the desires and wishes of the states considered relevant. Individuals became the property of the federal government. Soon the idea of direct taxation, forced federal military service and a myriad of other encroachments appeared.

In very real terms the War Between the States was a rebellion. It was a successful rebellion and resulted in a new form of government coming to power. Our history books teach that the Confederacy was rebellious against Constitutional principles. It was in fact the reconstructionist that succeeded in laying to rest the old Constitutional principles and the old Republic and replacing it with a strong federal government of their liking. The enactment of the 14th Amendment was the mechanism that gave teeth and power to this new government.

While federalist may wave the 14th Amendment and shout that this is the end of secession we hold up that document and proclaim it to be the primary justification for secession. It is on its face a bad amendment that contradicts the very principles of States Rights and checks on the power of the Federal government that were so carefully crafted into the Constitution. If this amendment were ratified in the ways and means properly set aside in the Constitution, we would disagree with it and wish to see it amended. This amendment was not ratified according to law; it was enacted contrary to all proper principles.

When this amendment was proposed there were thirty-seven states in the Union. This was of course during reconstruction and the thirteen states of the Confederacy were for all practical purposes not part of the Union. To avoid the indelicate position of declaring these states outside the Union when a war had just been fought to declare it impossible for them to leave the amendment was sent to all thirty-seven states.

In 1866 the states answer on the amendment was received in Washington. Of the twenty-eight states needed to ratify twenty-two voted for and thirteen voted against. The amendment was thus rejected according to the guidelines set forth in the Constitution.

Dissatisfied with this outcome the Congress; composed solely of representatives from the states that supported the amendment, declared that the thirteen Southern states that comprised the Confederacy were outside of the Union. It is ironic that by legislative feat the Congress accomplished what the Lincoln administration declared illegal just five years before. By ejecting the thirteen Southern states from the Union, again, the amendment was easily able to be ratified by the remaining states.

Easily ratified is probably too strong of a term. After Congress' action to eject the South from the Union Ohio, New Jersey and Oregon rescinded their ratifications of the amendment.

The South was faced with an impossible choice at this juncture. After being denied the right to leave the Union on their own volition the Federal Congress had ejected them and required acceptance of the new Constitution as a prerequisite for reentry. Faced with the option of perpetual occupation and the hope for partial autonomy each of the states eventually accepted the Constitution that was forced upon them.

Under such circumstances where is the consent of the governed? Where is the contract between the government and the people? The 14th Amendment created a very different Federal government with greatly expanded powers. It was never legally ratified; rather it was enacted and then forced upon an occupied people. Coercion and democracy do not make good bedfellows.

The issue of the illegitimacy of the 14th Amendment is not one of North versus South.

This is an issue of Constitutional principles and the legitimacy of government to govern. The methods used to enact this amendment and the tactics of extortion used to force acceptance of states and people opposed to it are pages torn directly from the history of any empire. The (il)legitimacy of the entire federal government rest on this action.

This is not a government of the people nor has it lived up to the original compact that gave it birth. The illegal and illegitimate enactment of the 14th Amendment is justification number one for secession and the establishment of a form of government of the people.

Recedite, plebes! Gero rem imperialem
El Cid

Was the Fourteenth Amendment Constitutionally Adopted?

By Dr. Forrest McDonald
1991

During and after the Civil War, Southerners repeatedly declared that the cause for which they fought was the "sublime moral principle" of states' rights. Given such protestations, and given the history of southern resistance to federal authority throughout the antebellum period, it is easy enough to associate states' rights exclusively with the South—but it is also mistaken. Connecticut and Massachusetts endorsed interposition in 1808; the Hartford Convention of 1814 did the same. In 1840 Vermont made it a crime to aid in the capture of a runaway slave, despite the federal fugitive slave act. In 1846 the Massachusetts House of Representatives declared the Mexican War unconstitutional; a decade later Wisconsin asserted the supremacy of its supreme court over the United States Supreme Court. [22]

Yet it was the seceding states that had carried the doctrine of states' rights to the extreme, and northern Radical Republicans, in their zeal to punish, plunder, and reconstruct the South, were willing to undermine the doctrine as part of their undertaking. Whatever else the Radicals had in mind in pushing through the Reconstruction Amendments—their motives were diverse and conflicting—it is clear that some of them, at least, intended that the Fourteenth should greatly increase the powers of Congress at the expense of the States. [23]

It is also clear that the process of adopting the Fourteenth Amendment was marred by repeated irregularities. President Andrew Johnson questioned the legitimacy of an amendment proposed by a Congress that represented only twenty-five of the thirty-six states. Three northern states that ratified the proposal later rescinded their votes. All the southern states except Tennessee at first voted against the amendment, despite an implied threat that they would not be readmitted to the Union; they changed their stands only after the threat was made explicit. And throughout the debates on the amendment, friends and foes alike disagreed as to whether approval of three-quarters of twenty-five states or of thirty-six would be necessary.

Ultimately, the issue would turn on the question whether the southern states had legally seceded. Both presidents Lincoln and Johnson and the Supreme Court held to the contrary. Radicals in Congress disagreed, but the Congress as a whole followed an inconsistent course. For all these reasons, the constitutionality of the adoption of the Fourteenth Amendment remains open to question.

Historiographic Background

The subject has a historiography, and not altogether a savory one. In 1953, after the first round of arguments in *Brown v. Board* and the other school desegregation cases, the Supreme Court ordered counsel to answer certain queries regarding various events connected with the adoption of the Fourteenth Amendment. The Court was specifically interested in the intent of the framers respecting segregation, but a Tulane law professor, Walter J. Suthon, Jr., responded by publishing an article questioning the "dubious origin" of the amendment. In it, he traced the origins of Article V, the amending clause of the Constitution, put together a brief history of the proposal of the amendment and its forced ratification in the South, and concluded that the intent of the framers was irrelevant, for the whole proceeding, start to finish, was unconstitutional.

In 1958, after the decision in *Brown v. Board* and amidst massive southern resistance to desegregation, a Houston lawyer named Pinckney G. McElwee published an article in the *South Carolina Law Quarterly* that reached the same conclusion. [24]   McElwee's study was more thorough than Suthon's had been, and he quoted from and cited more contemporary documents, but his piece was marred by a certain shrillness of tone.

Two years later, the *Georgia Bar Journal* published "a statement issued by the State Sovereignty Commission of Louisiana" entitled "*Unconstitutional Creation of the Fourteenth Amendment.*" [25]   The statement rehearsed the facts, garbling several of them along the way, called for the Supreme Court to declare the amendment illegal, and concluded that the amendment was mistitled and should be designated "Military Edict No. 1." *Baylor Law Review* produced a shorter - and more accurate and more moderate version of the argument in 1961, and the Alabama Lawyer reprinted that article in 1963.

All such efforts were directed against the desegregation decisions, and in 1966 a California lawyer named Ferdinand Fernandez took pen in hand to write a long and angry rebuttal. [26]

He succeeded in answering some of the critics' charges, but he misunderstood the main thrust of their arguments and ended up knocking over straw men. At that point legal scholars and historians largely abandoned the issue-though it occasionally cropped up in the literature for another two decades-and concentrated their efforts instead upon studying the intent of the framers.

They have generated a huge body of literature on that subject, but shed little light on the question of the constitutionality of the adoption procedure. Among such scholars, Alfred Avins, professor of law at Memphis State University, deserves special mention because of his herculean efforts in compiling a volume covering the legislative history and debates in Congress on all three Reconstruction amendments. [27]

Avins' volume is invaluable to anyone studying the origins of the Fourteenth Amendment, as are two studies by Joseph B. James. The first is *The Framing of the Fourteenth Amendment*, published in 1956. [28]

The second is a sequel, *The Ratification of the Fourteenth Amendment,* published in 1984. [29]   James is judicious and cautious, and he avoids drawing any conclusions about whether the amendment was constitutionally adopted, but he provides abundant material from which readers can draw their own conclusions.

Passage in Congress

To turn now to substantive aspects of the question, the first irregularity-the passage of the amendment by an incomplete Congress-can be disposed of rather briefly. The final vote in the House of Representatives was 120 to 32, with 32 abstentions-far more than the requisite two-thirds majority. [30] But the eleven states of the erstwhile Confederacy were entitled to and had elected 61 representatives who had been denied seats [31], all of whom would doubtless have voted in the negative. Had their votes been cast, the majority would have been only 56 percent. Besides, the majority included representatives from the newly admitted states of West Virginia and Nevada, the constitutionality of whose statehood was doubtful. In the Senate a similar situation pertained. The vote there was 33 to 11, with 5 abstentions. [32] If the twenty-two seats of the former Confederate states were added in the negative column, there would have been a tie vote, and if the four seats held by West Virginia and Nevada were subtracted from the affirmative column, the aye votes would have fallen short of even a simple majority.

But that does not exhaust the question. Article V provides that "Congress, whenever two-thirds of both Houses shall deem it necessary, shall propose Amendments." The wording is not explicit as to whether "two-thirds of both Houses" means two-thirds of the members or two-thirds of those present and voting. But Article I, Section 5, defines a quorum as a simple majority, gives each house power to judge the qualifications of its members, and authorizes each to make its own rules. It follows logically that when the Thirty-ninth Congress approved the Fourteenth Amendment in 1866 by more than two-thirds of the members present in each house, it was acting within the framework of the rules as established in the Constitution.

There was ample precedent for so reasoning. Though the records do not itemize the voting in the First Congress on the amendments that became the Bill of Rights, it is clear from the debates that the members read "two-thirds of both Houses" to mean two-thirds of a quorum. [33]   When the Twelfth Amendment was under discussion fourteen years later, the subject was debated at length. The Senate passed the measure by more than two-thirds of those present, but by one vote less than two-thirds of the whole membership; over the objections of the minority, Vice-president Aaron Burr ruled that the majority was adequate. When the House took up the proposal, the same objection was raised, with an ingenious twist. It was pointed out that in the other instances in which the Constitution requires two-thirds majorities, in impeachment trials (Article I,. Section 3) and in ratifying treaties (Article II, Section 2), the language is "two thirds of the Members present" and "of the Senators present," and some Representatives inferred that the different phraseology in Article V thereby meant two-thirds of the whole body. The House, however, overwhelmingly rejected the argument. [34]

But another aspect of the matter clouds the issue. The numbers cited concerning the vote in the Senate mask some chicanery. One of the fifty non-southern senators was the newly elected John P. Stockton of New Jersey, an outspoken opponent of the Fourteenth Amendment, who took the oath of office and was formally seated when the Thirty-ninth Congress convened on December 5, 1865. Later, after informal polls revealed that only thirty-three senators favored it (one short of the necessary two-thirds) a motion was made not to seat Stockton. The motion not to seat was resorted to, even though he had already been seated, because Article I, Section 5, of the Constitution, requires a two-thirds vote to expel a member, and that majority could not be mustered. Following a great deal of debate, a vote was taken and the motion not to seat failed twenty-two to twenty-one. Overnight, however, one member of the Senate was persuaded to change his vote. The next day the same motion passed. Stockton was thus unconstitutionally expelled, and only in that way did the thirty-three votes for the Fourteenth Amendment become a two-thirds majority.[35]

Early Ratifications and Rejections

Even more vexing questions arise when we consider the process of ratification. Senator Charles Sumner of Massachusetts had, as early as 1862, formulated his "state suicide" theory, which held that the very act of seceding destroyed a state and dissolved its lawful government. In the House the Radical Pennsylvanian Thaddeus Stevens advanced the alternate theory that the eleven southern states were conquered provinces without any political rights.

Either way, the ex-Confederates were governable exclusively by Congress under its express power to govern territories and could have no voice in ratifying amendments. Accordingly, nineteen of the twenty-five loyal states would constitute the three-fourths majority necessary to ratify the Fourteenth Amendment, not twenty-seven of thirty-six states counting the South.

Congress might have had the right to act on either theory, but instead, it rejected both. What is more, on June 16, 1866, when the proposed amendment was sent to the state governors for legislative ratification, it was sent to all thirty-six, a tacit endorsement of the position that the southern states were still full-fledged members of the Union. [36]   Against that ambiguous background, the contests over ratification got off to an erratic start. Five states ratified within the first three months. Ratification by Connecticut, New Hampshire, and New Jersey was unexceptional, though the vote in New Jersey was close and the state would later rescind its ratification; but the action in Tennessee and Oregon was most irregular. Opponents of the amendment in the Tennessee House absented themselves, preventing a quorum. Two absent members were forcibly seized, a criminal court ordered them released by a writ of *habeas corpus*, the House ignored the writ, and the two were held in an anteroom. The speaker declared them absent and ruled that there was no quorum, but he was overruled by the members present. What was essentially a rump House then proceeded to vote for ratification. [37]

Ratification in Oregon was equally irregular. Republicans in the state (who like most Republicans everywhere favored ratification) had a majority of one in the state's House of Representatives, but two of their seats were challenged. The two were temporarily seated and provided a narrow margin for ratification. Later in the session, however, the disputed seats were awarded to Democrats on the ground that the Republicans had been illegally elected, whereupon the legislature rescinded its ratification. [38]

Late in October Vermont added its ratification, but then the southern states began to be heard from-loudly and negatively. On October 27, 1866, Texas voted overwhelmingly not to ratify, the House by a seventy to five majority, the Senate by twenty-seven to one. Significantly, the legislature pledged its loyalty to the Constitution and promised to abide by the Fourteenth Amendment if it should be ratified by the necessary proportion of the other states. Georgia followed the same course two weeks later, its Senate unanimously, its House with only two votes in favor of ratification. [39]

In December more southern states rejected the amendment, and a portentous note was heard from a loyal state. The Florida House voted unanimously against ratification on December 1, the Senate unanimously against ratification two days later. In mid-month Arkansas, North Carolina, and South Carolina followed suit, in every instance by huge majorities. About the same time, friends of the amendment were handed another disappointment: Governor F. F. Low of California, though a Republican, refused to call a special session of the legislature to consider the amendment. California would subsequently reject it. [40]

As Radicals in Congress began to discuss revisions of the amendment and draconian measures to secure its adoption, more rejections came during January of 1867. Virginia summarily voted against the amendment early in the month; Alabama, after having debated it longer than any other state, also voted no; and toward the end of the month Mississippi did likewise. Louisiana followed early in February. What was more, two loyal border states, Kentucky and Delaware, had joined the ranks of those rejecting the proposed amendment. A third loyal border state, Maryland, would do so in March. [41]

In sum, as the last days of the Thirty-ninth Congress approached-I t would expire on March 4, 1867-Fourteenth Amendment appeared to be doomed. The admission of Nebraska to statehood on March 1 brought the number of states to thirty-seven, meaning that twenty-eight states would be required for ratification if the southern states were counted. But eleven had already voted no, and Maryland would make it twelve.

Changing the Rules

Yet a course of action remained whereby Congress could have brought about ratification at least marginally within the boundaries of the Constitution. Article I, Section 8, empowers Congress to determine whether a domestic insurrection is taking place, and under Article IV, Section 4, the United States guarantees each state a republican form of government and protects each against invasion or domestic violence guarantees and protections that, according to the Supreme Court's subsequent ruling, were primarily "legislative."

The proclamation by President Johnson on August 20, 1866, that the rebellion had ended in all states and that "peace, order, tranquility and civil authority now exist in and throughout the whole of the United States" could, therefore, have only "provisional" force until Congress acted. Moreover, though the Supreme Court would hold in Texas v. White (1869) that the Constitution "looks to an indestructible Union, composed of indestructible States," it remained bound by its prior ruling in Luther v. Borden (1849) that matters of the legitimacy of state regimes arising under the republican government guarantee clause were "political questions" falling under the exclusive control of Congress and not subject to adjudication in the courts. [42]

The inescapable conclusion from these considerations is that Congress would have faced no constitutional barriers had it embraced either Sumner's state-suicide theory or Stevens' conquered-province theory. Having done so, it could then have proclaimed that the Fourteenth Amendment would be officially ratified whenever twenty of the twenty-six "legitimate" or loyal states (including Nebraska) had approved. Subsequently, it could require the erstwhile southern states to approve the Constitution, including the new amendment, as a condition of admission to statehood, just as it could in admitting more conventional territories.

There is a complication in this scenario. Kentucky, Delaware, and Maryland, as we have seen, rejected the proposed amendment outright, and California did so later. Ohio, New Jersey, and Oregon rescinded their ratifications. If the rescissions were allowed, only nineteen states, not the requisite twenty, would have ratified. When introduced in Congress, however, the rescissions were rejected, despite the argument that a legislative ratification of an amendment was not a contract until it became part of the Constitution and could, therefore, be canceled. Though the question is a sticky one, over which there is still disagreement, Congress was the final arbiter in the matter. The Supreme Court never ruled on the question directly, though in later cases, concerning different amendments, it declared that Congress necessarily had the last word. [43]

Interestingly, it was the Radicals who proposed to follow the constitutional way of bringing about approval of the amendment-not because they had strong constitutional scruples, but because they wanted to keep the southern states out of the Union until further reforms could be imposed upon them, including suffrage for the freedmen and a general redistribution of all property. Instead, "moderate" and "conservative" Republicans prevailed, resulting in ratification of the Fourteenth Amendment by means that cannot be squared with either the Constitution or the Republicans' own internal logic. [44]

A Coercive Procedure

The congressional majority used the Reconstruction Act of March 2, 1867, passed over President Johnson's veto just before the expiration of the Thirty-ninth Congress and slightly amended by the Fortieth Congress later the same month, to force the southern states to approve the amendment. The act, as amended, began with a declaration that "no legal state governments" existed in the ten "rebel" states that had refused to ratify. It divided the South into five military districts and replaced the existing governmental structures with martial law. The act required the "rebel" states to call elections, in which black males could vote, but whites who had participated in the rebellion or given aid and comfort to rebels could not.

Thus the states would elect delegates to conventions that were to establish constitutions that included provisions for black suffrage. [45] When the constitutions were ratified by a majority of the eligible voters and approved by Congress, when governments were organized under them, and when those governments ratified the Fourteenth Amendment, then-and only then-would Congress consider ending military rule, recognizing the state governments as legally existent and readmitting the states to representation in Congress. [46]

The act flew in the face of the Constitution in a large variety of ways. First, it ran counter to the decision of the Supreme Court in *Ex parte* Milligan. [47] Less than three months earlier, the Court had ruled that martial law could not constitutionally be imposed, in the absence of war or rebellion, in areas where the civilian courts were functioning. Next, in its peculiar holding that the states had continued to exist but were without legal government, the act entangled itself in contradictions. All the involved states except Mississippi, which had extensively amended its 1832 constitution, had drafted new constitutions under the auspices and with the approval of the federal government. Louisiana, for example, had adopted its constitution in 1864 under suggestions and directions from President Lincoln. And, tellingly, Congress had called upon the legislatures elected under those constitutions to ratify the Thirteenth Amendment in 1865. The votes of six of them -Alabama, Arkansas, Georgia, North Carolina, South Carolina, and Tennessee-were counted as being among the three-fourths majority. In other words, in 1865 Congress had recognized the legitimacy of the southern state governments for purposes of ratifying the Thirteenth Amendment, but, though nothing about those governments had changed by 1867, Congress denied their legitimacy when they voted to reject the Fourteenth Amendment.

Next, as President Johnson said in his veto message, the act deprived most white southerners of their political and civil rights on a wholesale basis, without due process of law, in violation of the Fifth Amendment. Moreover, it effectively served as "a bill of attainder against 9,000,000 people at once," all of whom were excluded from a hearing through their representatives, on the basis of "an accusation so vague as to be scarcely intelligible and found to be true upon no credible evidence." Further, the preclusion of southern representation in Congress by statute distorted one feature of the Constitution to annul two other features. Article I, Section 5, which declares that "Each House shall be the Judge of the Elections, Returns and Qualifications of its own members," clearly contemplates the judging of each member individually, through hearings and the taking of evidence. Yet by arbitrarily excluding members from specified states, Congressmen were not judging; they were refusing to judge. By doing so, they deprived the designated states of their constitutional rights to representation as provided by Article I, Sections 2 and 3, and Article V.

Finally, the coercive quality of the act made it unconstitutional as well. Several sets of aims underlay the coerciveness, but Senator James Doolittle of Wisconsin certainly identified one of them when he said that "the people of the South have rejected the constitutional amendment," and we will, therefore "march upon them and force them to adopt it at the point of the bayonet" and rule them with military force "until they do adopt it." [48]

The Supreme Court Declines to Intervene

In response to the Reconstruction Act and its supplementary legislation, the South challenged them in the Supreme Court. The South had grounds for hoping that the Court would strike down the legislation, for it had faced up to Congress in the Milligan case and had recently overturned state and federal loyalty oaths; but the hope turned out to be ill-founded. Mississippi led off by seeking an injunction against President Johnson and the district military commander, restraining them from executing and enforcing the acts. The Court declined on the ground that it lacked the power. Then Georgia brought a suit against Secretary of War Edwin Stanton, General Ulysses S. Grant, and the commander of the Third Military District, seeking a similar injunction on the ground that Congress had no power to annihilate a state government and thereby deprive its citizens of legal and political rights. The Court declined, holding that for a question to be judicially determined, "the rights in danger ... must be rights of persons or property, not merely political rights, which do not belong to the jurisdiction of a court." [49]

This language hinted broadly that if a suit were brought on an issue of property rights, the Court would hear it and rule on the constitutionality of the Reconstruction Acts. Such a case, *Ex parte* McCardle, was brought early in 1868, and the Court heard arguments in March, just before the impeachment trial of President Johnson got underway. In that highly charged atmosphere Congress passed, as a rider to a bill regarding appeals in customs and revenue cases, a measure removing the Court's jurisdiction in the McCardle case. That, for practical purposes, killed all prospects of a judicial overthrow of the Reconstruction Acts. [50]

Despairing of stopping the congressional juggernaut, ruled by military commanders who removed governors and judges at will, and swept by rumors that Congress intended to confiscate and redistribute their property (as some Radicals indeed did), the southern states began to capitulate. The ambience is captured in the journals of the House and Senate of Louisiana for the opening day of their sessions in late June 1868. The proceedings began with the reading of orders from General Grant, stressing the supremacy of the army over the "provisional" civil government, established in accordance with the Reconstruction Act. Armed federal soldiers milled around outside. They were still there when the puppet legislature voted to ratify the Fourteenth Amendment ten days later.

Southerners made some feeble attempts at resistance. In February Alabama whites had sought to prevent the adoption of a constitution that was being forced on them under the Reconstruction Act. Using a tactic contemplated in other states as well, they stayed away from the polls to prevent the new constitution from being approved by a majority of the registered voters. Of the 170,631 registered voters, fewer than 71,000 turned out; and though 69,807 of these voted to ratify, that was less than a majority. Congress responded by promptly repealing the majority-of-the-voters requirement and allowing a bare majority of votes cast to suffice. [51]

Ratification: The Essential Contradiction

We now come to the pivotal point upon which the constitutionality of the adoption of the Fourteenth Amendment turns. Let us assume that the amendment had been constitutionally proposed; assume that the ratifications in Tennessee, Oregon, and West Virginia were proper and should have been counted; and assume that the rescissions by New Jersey and Ohio were illegal and that their ratifications should be counted. Even so, as of April 1, 1868, the approval of six more states was necessary to validate the amendment. Let us further assume that the Reconstruction Act of March 2, 1867, was constitutional, and that ratification by the governments of the reconstituted southern states would count toward the necessary total.

Even if we make all these assumptions, it remains a fact that the southern state governments could have a voice in ratifying the amendment only if they were duly recognized as governments at the time they acted on the amendment. Congress had taken it upon itself-properly or improperly, it does not matter for present purposes-to be the arbiter of whether the governments were legitimate.

Now let us see.

Arkansas was the first to act. It adopted its new state constitution on April 1, 1868. Two days later the legislature considered the Fourteenth Amendment, and by April 6 both houses had voted for ratification. But no resolution to recognize the loyalty of Arkansas's government was proposed in Congress until May 7, and the resolution was not adopted until mid-June. Therefore, the vote on the Fourteenth Amendment had been taken by a state which, under the congressional act of March 2, 1867, still had "no legal state government." [52]

Next came Florida, which in May 1868, approved a new constitution that had been drafted by a convention presided over by Colonel John Sprague of the United States Army, in full military uniform. The new legislature met in June and, "as dictated by the Acts of Congress as conditions precedent to admission," ratified the amendment on June 9. But a problem arose when Congress debated whether to readmit the state: it turned out that the wording of the amendment as adopted by Florida differed in several particulars from the phraseology proposed by Congress.

Some senators objected that Florida had therefore not properly adopted the amendment. After some desultory discussion, Senator Frederick Frelinghausen of New Jersey checked the ratifications of four states chosen at random-New York, Pennsylvania, Michigan, and Wisconsin-and reported that none had ratified the amendment exactly as proposed by Congress. "In the ratification by Wisconsin," he said, "in one sentence, there were four or five errors," some of them substantive. He added that if he examined the ratifications of all the states, he would probably "find like inaccuracies in each certificate." Instead of ruling that no state had properly ratified, however, Congress decided that ratification in any form was acceptable; and Florida was accordingly readmitted to statehood as a "legal government."

At that point, Congress changed the rules somewhat. Heretofore, ratification of the Fourteenth Amendment had been a necessary qualification for readmission to statehood, but not a sufficient one, which is to say that after the non-government of a state ratified, Congress would consider readmission. An act passed June 25, 1868, altered the procedure. The preamble of the act declared that several southern states had "framed constitutions of State government which are republican"; article one enacted that each of them "shall be entitled and admitted to representation in Congress as a State of the Union" automatically when they ratified the amendment. Obviously, however, they were not states at the time they ratified, for if they were, they would already have been "entitled" to representation.

On those terms, North Carolina voted to ratify on July 2, South Carolina and Louisiana on July 9, and Alabama on July 16. According to the tally kept by Secretary of State William H. Seward, that made twenty-eight states, and on July 20 he proclaimed the amendment to be ratified. After some wrangling over who had the authority to determine, Congress confirmed its adoption.

Conclusion

Clearly, then, the Fourteenth Amendment was never constitutionally ratified, even if it had been constitutionally proposed. The question now becomes, so what? The critics of the 1950s and 1960s, cited earlier, called for the Supreme Court to rule that it was, not a part of the Constitution. To the certain objection that such a ruling would overturn a huge body of judicial precedent, they pointed out that the Court had, in Erie v. Tompkins (1938), overturned its earlier ruling in Swift v. Tyson (1842) and with it nearly a century of case law, and that to right a long-standing wrong was more important than precedent. Perhaps. Even so, though no one ever became rich by predicting what the Supreme Court would do from one generation to another, it seems safe to predict that the Fourteenth Amendment is here to stay, despite its origins. It behooves us, however, to be aware of the Fourteenth's history, lest similar irregularities should surround another amendment in the future.

This article was originally published in the *Georgia Journal of Southern Legal History* in 1991.

Republished via The Abbeville Institute Apr, 23, 2014. Sadly Dr. McDonald passed Jan. 19, 2016 and permission was not secured from him to include his work here. It is included with commentary below under the Fair Use Doctrine with the highest respect and regard for his work and ideas.

Secessionist No. 5: Commentary

By Barry Lee Clark

The two essays above should leave the reader with no doubt that the history of the 14th Amendment is at the very least extraordinary and odd. Dr. Forrest McDonald's piece alone, considering his qualifications and eminence in the field, ought to be enough to persuade most that there is vigor in his claim. However, to make a call for such would be simply a matter of creating a fallacy of arguing from authority. There are, after all, numerous "authorities" that simply ignore the undeniable historic truths related to this issue and make claims counter to the arguments presented above. If it is insufficient to state that Dr. McDonald was certainly qualified and competent in his position to make this argument and that the argument itself is logically placed and historically accurate we are left to highlight some of the points made therein in order to prove its worth.

In a paper entitled *"The First War of the New Order"*, I argued that the enactment of the 14th Amendment was the culmination of a fundamental change in government in America that was intentional and deliberate and after the events of 1861-1870 the form of government looked the same after but it was radically different in function. [53] And, that the means utilized to achieve the ends of this new form of government were contrary to the established rule of law, custom and common understanding.

To merely state that the means used were unorthodox is an understatement for they consisted of deceit, extortion and rewriting the rules as the process went along – regardless of law or common sense.

After ratifying the 13th Amendment in 1865 Southern state representatives to Congress found themselves denied entry and their states declared not to have legitimate governments because their states had refused to ratify the 14th Amendment, essentially the Southern states were considered to not be part of the Union since their secession in 1861. [54]   This situation created an obvious paradox, if the Southern states were no longer part of the Union they had the obvious right to leave in 1861. If they could not leave then they were still part of the Union, they had ratified the 13th amendment two years prior, in this case, the motion under Article V of the Constitution to propose the 14th Amendment could never have passed in the first place. [55] It was not just the entire Southern delegation that was excluded, Senator John Stockton from New Jersey who opposed the 14th Amendment was denied his seat. [56]

Then, of course, there is the matter of the events in Tennessee, Ohio, Oregon and New Jersey related to either their dubious ratification or attempts to rescind their votes for the amendment before it was made law, all covered in detail in the articles above. Finally, there is the matter that the Southern States were forced, essentially at gunpoint under military occupation, to agree to the amendment.

The essays above make a strong, historical and logical case that: the 14th Amendment was not properly proposed according to Article V of the Constitution and once proposed the ratification process was fraught with irregularities and actions contrary to law. As Dr. Tom Woods says, in the very recent past the invalidity of this amendment was common knowledge, now this is treated as a quack theory. [57]   As late at 1957, an article in the US News and World Report, titled "There is No Fourteenth Amendment", validated that this was an idea that existed in the mainstream. [58]

One has to wonder how such provable historical facts, articulated by a qualified man such as Dr. McDonald can be ignored by other "authorities".

Truth is sometimes a nasty business it seems when it is contrary to the narrative people want to paint.

Second Edition Commentary
By Barry Lee Clark

One of my primary motivations for updating and revising the work of the first edition was to keep the work of Dr. Forrest MacDonald in the public sphere. His 1991 article above published in the *Georgia Journal of Southern Legal History* should be required reading of every high school and college student in an American government class and the facts and conclusions he presents should be part of every first-year law program in the United States.

Three factors bring me to that conclusion. First, the Fourteenth Amendment so fundamentally changed the nature of the government in the United States it is worthy of more study than any other portion of the Constitution. Since it is so critically important to all the Federal government does, via the self-created incorporation doctrine, it is vital to understand its history. Second, we believe ourselves a nation of laws. This is the most transformational language within our codified law. If it was improperly enacted, as Dr. MacDonald proves, this is a significant disconnect between who we think we are, what we think our government is and reality. Lastly, nobody previous or since has articulated the arguments related to this charade of law as clearly nor as powerfully as Dr. MacDonald.

Secessionist No. 6: Were the States Sovereign?

by Brian McCandliss
April 20, 2004

A defining – but so far unasked – question regarding the Civil War is the political status of the states: specifically, was the "United States of America" indeed, as our popular Pledge of Allegiance claims, "one nation, indivisible?" Or was it, rather, a union of sovereign nations, bound only to each other by mere treaty, as with any other treaty – such as the current United Nations? (As a point of fact, the term "union" is the only term used in the text of the Constitution to refer to the United States, while the word "nation" never appears a single time).

This question seems to be the proverbial "elephant in the room" of American law and history, for its answer is key in defining a state's right of secession: this question marks the difference between, for example, Boston seceding from Massachusetts, and Spain seceding from the United Nations. While in the first instance, few would question the legal right of state officials to use force in preventing local urban inhabitants from seceding with a state's city, such an exercise against a sovereign nation in the latter example would be (hopefully) viewed as nothing short of ruthless imperialism equivalent to that of Saddam Hussein, Adolph Hitler or Genghis Khan.

As such, similar implications accrue to United States President Abraham Lincoln from this question, in appraising him as either an upholder of law or a dictator, regarding his particular instance in history of using military force. If on the one hand, the states were held – by law – irrevocably to the Union, then Lincoln would have simply been performing his sworn duty as necessary under extreme conditions, and his defenders might have firm ground in excusing his having "bent a few rules" to get the job done.

If, however, the states were indeed separate nations, then this would define Lincoln as both the ultimate traitor, and most ruthless imperialist of his time, via breaching his oaths to defend the existing order of a self-defined republic of separate nations in order to overturn it in favor of what fits the official definition of an "empire;" likewise, his defenders and supporters would likewise classify as both similarly ruthless power seekers, and what Lenin termed "useful idiots."

To resolve this dichotomy, we must examine the relevant facts:

Lincoln claimed in his famous First Inaugural Address that "no State upon its own mere motion can lawfully get out of the Union." He could only have been referring to "the Union" as set forth in the Constitution; for, prior to this, there can be no disputing the fact that the states were free and sovereign nations – as established in the Articles of Confederation, which under Article II states that:

"Each state retains its sovereignty, freedom, and independence, and every power, jurisdiction, and right, which is not by this Confederation expressly delegated to the United States, in Congress assembled."

Here the term "delegated" requires contextual definition, meaning literally "to make lesser law;" when powers are "delegated," they are merely passed down a chain-of-command to a subordinate agent by a superior principal authority, in order to provide that agent with representative "proxy" authority to carry out respective duties. In no way may does this delegated authority ever supersede or negate that of the delegating body – any more than a company employee who is delegated authority by his manager, can give orders to the firm's owner, or override the dictates of such. Rather, such a representative can be overridden at any time at the behest of the superior – or discharged entirely.

As such, a "delegation" clause cannot be seen as a compromise or surrender of sovereignty in any way.

Thus, the force and effectiveness of this sovereignty which was thus "retained" from the Declaration of Independence, was equivalent to that of any other nation; this was made clear in the Declaration, via the statement:

"That these United Colonies are, and of right ought to be, FREE AND INDEPENDENT STATES; that they are absolved from all allegiance to the British crown and that all political connection between them and the state of Great Britain is, and ought to be, totally dissolved; and that, as free and independent states, they have full power to levy war, conclude peace, contract alliances, establish commerce, and do all other acts and things which independent states may of right do" (emphasis in original).

(Note that the term "state" used here in the Declaration, is clearly used synonymously with the term "nation" for the purposes of this document; as such, the United States had no more claim in binding South Carolina or Virginia, than it had in binding England or France, and the term "United States" literally meant "United Nations.")

Lincoln and his defenders, then, must believe that the states somehow "surrendered" their status as sovereign nations, in the act of ratifying the Constitution (or, as Lincoln added in his First Inaugural, "the union matured"). However, this is negated by the 10th Amendment specification that powers were merely delegated, i.e.,

"The powers not delegated to the United States by the Constitution, nor prohibited by it to the states, are **reserved to the states respectively, or to the people**" (emphasis added).

In this context, therefore, powers were delegated to the federal government via the Constitution by the states ratifying it, not out in the interest of any sort of collectivism, but merely for the purposes of practical harmony in co-existence – with both union and non-union nations – solely for advancing the individual benefit of the respective delegating state.

Meanwhile, the 9th amendment likewise states that:

"The enumeration in the Constitution, of certain rights, shall not be construed to deny or disparage others retained by the people."

Since the term "others" as used here, clearly refers to rights not enumerated in the text of the Constitution, then it thus implicitly preserves those rights enumerated via prior documents – such as the Articles of Confederation, which specifically retains the "sovereignty, freedom and independence" of every state – which the Constitution does not exclude anywhere (but rather preserves, since states would have to retain their sovereign powers in order to delegate them).

Here the term "the people" must likewise be defined, with this term referring to the same "people" referenced initially in the Constitution's preamble – and which, as has been well-established elsewhere, did not refer to all persons in the United States collectively; rather, the term "the people" refers solely to the citizens of the states individually and respectively, speaking through their elected officials – and even then, only those states ratifying the Constitution at the time.

This is further implied in the Constitution's Article IV, Section 2, statement that:

"The citizens of each state shall be entitled to all privileges and immunities of citizens in the several states."

Clearly, separate reference to "citizens of each state," as opposed to "citizens in the several states," clarifies that citizenship was strictly state-specific and derived, and not union-related in any way whatsoever: in fact, the term "Citizen of the United States" was never known prior to the passage of the 14th amendment following the Civil War – being a pure post-Lincoln invention – , and would have no more meaning prior to that war, than "Citizen of the United Nations" in today's context to imply similar supremacy.

As such, it is clear that the Ninth Amendment implicitly reserved the right of every state, to the same sovereignty, freedom and independence which existed previously, i.e., no less than that of any other nation in the world.

Finally, even when admitting all of the above, anti-secessionists almost unanimously claim their proverbial "trump-card" in the Constitution's so-called "Supremacy clause" of U.S. Constitution Article VI, which states that:

"This Constitution... shall be the Supreme Law of the Land, and the judges in every state shall be bound thereby, anything in the laws or constitutions of any state notwithstanding."

The level of absurdity in declaring any sort of logical victory, based on such an obviously flawed argument is astounding; for here the explicit language regarding this "Supreme Law" clearly, specifically and unmistakably states – in plain English, no less – that this "law" is binding on "the judges in every state – " and only the judges.

In contrast, the remainder of the Article omits all other officials from any such bond, using very different language in describing its relation to them; to wit:

"The Senators and Representatives before mentioned, and the members of the several state legislatures, and all executive and judicial officers, both of the United States and of the several states, shall be bound by oath or affirmation, to support this Constitution; but no religious test shall ever be required as a qualification to any office or public trust under the United States."

Any person literate in the English language – not to mention the language of law and logic – should be able to recognize that such explicitly omissive and separate treatment, translates to the fact that the Constitution does not claim any legally binding effect whatsoever, on anyone but state judges; rather, such language merely implies recognition of the Constitution by officials as a mere mutual good-faith agreement. It is simply absurd, after all, to claim that the phrase "state judges shall be bound by law, while all others shall be bound merely by a promise or agreement to support the law," somehow translates to the notion that "all officials are bound by law – " particularly when the final clause specifically precludes any religious test from implying the term "oath or affirmation" as binding via any common "higher law," such as an oath specifically to God, Allah or the Buddha – even allowing religions for which oath or affirmation has no higher context.

As such, the implication here is that the Constitution is a mere treaty between separate and sovereign nation-states – a treaty which state officials simply agree to "support," as opposed to being bound to obey such as a law, under penalty of such. Rather, this treaty is written as merely a bilateral agreement, with each side bound solely by its own conscience and good reputation – and as such, may be thus dispensed with entirely, if either side believes a breach of faith has been committed by the other.

To claim otherwise, i.e., that every state committed itself to the supreme and final binding arbitration (and mercy) of the Federal government in settling disputes – under force of law wielded by such – would not only be nonsensical for the purposes of protecting the states from possible abuses by this same Federal government, but moreover is nowhere expressed – or even implied – in the Constitution or any other document.

With the Constitution thus expressing nothing contrary to individual states retaining their status as sovereign nations, Lincoln found it thus necessary to invent such, claiming in his First Inaugural Address that "Perpetuity is implied, if not expressed, in the fundamental law of all national governments."

Here Lincoln commits a pure logical fallacy – if not an outright deception – via switching context and assuming, outright, that the Constitution defines a "national government." This assumption is not supported in the Constitution nor prior documents, but in fact his statement "implied if not expressed" specifically contradicts Ninth and Tenth Amendment reservations that all un-expressed rights and powers – including those of state sovereignty, freedom and independence – were retained by the states; even expressed powers of the United States were likewise mere delegations of state authority – thus implying their status as separate sovereign nations.

In conclusion, I cannot imagine why anyone would imagine that separate nations, would knowingly and willingly surrender their individual sovereignty – particularly, as in the case of the United States, after their having just won it via bloodshed from centralized and consolidated tyranny firsthand, against all believed likelihood of success; perhaps such persons believe Lincoln's claim – which he makes in his First Inaugural Address once again – that "All the vital rights of minorities and of individuals are so plainly assured to them by affirmations and negations, guaranties [sic] and prohibitions, in the Constitution that controversies never arise concerning them".

In like manner, I cannot answer how any rational or thinking person can be so naive, as to actually believe that any laws or order can be made so perfect as to preclude any incidence whatsoever of government breaches or excesses – to the extent of such "never arising" – so that the supreme protection of national sovereignty was no longer considered necessary or even desirable to the people of any state in the Union. Rather, I can only prove that such supreme national sovereignty was established and recognized by law for each and every state – and that no law or document that surrendered or compromised it in any manner whatsoever, was ever passed or ratified by them.

Brian McCandliss is a business and economics graduate of Liberty University in Lynchburg, VA, a law student, and a businessman in Detroit, Michigan

Originally posted on lewrockwell.com, included in the collection of Secessionist Papers with the express consent and support of the author

Secessionist No. 16: Addendum to No. 6

by Brian McCandliss June 2005

In my article "In my article "Were the States Sovereign Nations?" - Secessionist Paper No. 6, I concluded that the states were, indeed, separate sovereign nations under the law prior to the Civil War. Since this time, however, I have likewise come to a more-recent conclusion, i.e. that, legally speaking, that the states are still sovereign nations under the law.

This is because the Civil War was federally-proclaimed as a legal police-action to put down an unlawful rebellion, which it claimed was justified under an alleged legal-claim to federal national authority over the individual states. However, since this claim was legally false-- and, more importantly, since no laws were changed afterward to substantiate such a claim-- then it was merely an act of Orwellian censorship, i.e. an act by government in order to change the perceived meaning of the law via long-term totalitarian suppression of the truth.

As such, the current order of federal national authority over the individual states, is simply supported by repression-- not law. Rather, the law-- being, once again, unchanged from its original form with regards to state sovereignty-- still regards each state as a separate, sovereign nation unto itself (as stated above). Therefore, claims of the type that "Union victory ended forever the claim that state sovereignty superseded federal authority", are entirely spurious and fallacious; for the question is one of simple historical fact, not subsequent military victory. And no amount of force or victory can change or determine prior history, but rather can only suppress accurate readings and teachings thereof. History may be written by the victors, but it cannot be changed by such--- at least not without time-travel.

In conclusion, therefore, the states currently exist, legally speaking, under an order of pure suppression, whereby their true legal rights and status as separate, sovereign nations- equal to that of any other nation to be free from coercion by the US government-- are censored via ongoing occupation, backed up by threat of military retaliation for dissent or disobedience by any state.

Any serious discussion of "liberty" must recognize this fact concerning the current state-of-affairs under which we live-- as well as to recognize that the states are still sovereign nations under the law.

Secessionist No. 7: Considering Secession

by Michael Peirce, November 20, 2000

Mr. Brian Puckett of "Citizens of America" recently sent me a copy of an article by him that was published on the Sierra Times website. Mr. Puckett is a thoughtful and patriotic man, a leader in the struggle to preserve our constitutional right to own firearms. Sierra Times is a first-class website for people who value freedom.

Why then, do I choose to debate the issue of secession with Mr. Puckett? Well, for one thing, he is against it. The title of his essay was "Secession is Not the Best Solution." Here is his opinion on the matter:

"Before it is all lost, before we are subjugated by socialists, before the last vestiges of Constitutional rule are subverted, should we divide the country into states dominated by the two divergent factions? No, we should not. We should instead drive the socialists out of our schools, out of our government, and out of our lives."

Since I respect his well-reasoned arguments and am aware of his deep commitment to the cause of freedom, I gave the issue some more thought, facing the infinitely difficult task of trying to think like someone who doesn't agree with me. To do this it was necessary to take the approach that secession is a bad idea. It hurts just to write those words! Yet it wasn't hard to come up with a lot of reasons why this might be true. As an exercise, let's look at the issue from that point of view.

First, the obvious one – our first experiment with secession nearly drowned the country in blood. Hundreds of thousands of the best men in America died or were maimed in a war that devastated the South for decades and left many a family on both sides in mourning for years. Yet it must always be remembered – it was Northern troops, under the auspices of an out of control central government, who invaded the South. What choice was there for Southerners? Sometimes it really is necessary to fight. The question that confronts us is twofold, would it come to that? And if so, is it worth it?

There are administrative issues as well. What of the Federal government programs? What of the media? Who gets what? (I don't want Sam Donaldson!) What of the military, particularly the nuclear weapons? Who would get the aircraft carriers? How soon could we break up that communist teacher's union and bring the schools back on board, teaching our values? Would there be civil disorder?

These are serious issues and must be considered.

Having done so, it always comes back to same old questions. How can long can we tolerate this cesspool into which we and our children have been dragged? We have pretty graphic evidence that the Democratic party, the party of socialism, depravity, abortion and treason, will do virtually anything to retain control of the government apparatus. They already have control of the media and the schools. It is equally true that about one-third of our population supports them, and that demographic is, unfortunately, distributed throughout the country. While heavily concentrated along the coasts, it's a safe bet that some of these folks are living in our neighborhoods as well. Splitting this thing up would not be easy.

Yet we all have seen the map displaying the voter breakdown by county. The population that votes democratic is heavily massed on the coastal cities and some of the more porous areas of the border with Mexico. What a surprise.

Never was the cultural divide more graphically obvious. We, the cultural conservatives and "joe six-packs" of "flyover country" went overwhelmingly for Bush. We didn't love him – we were voting against the Democrats. We want our country back and voted accordingly. The cultural Marxists however, are very close to winning. Most of the people who live on entitlements, work for the government, the media or otherwise suck at the public trough, voted to continue re-distributing our wealth at the expense of our republic.

Academia, that haven for the very communistic theories rejected by the rest of the civilized world, went heavily for cultural Marxists; many if not most of the bigger colleges must be considered training grounds for the enemy. When one thinks of Marxism in the context of our colleges, it is hard to determine if we should be thinking of Karl or Groucho! We have a lot of house cleaning to do right in our own backyards, and since we can't just shoot all these lame brains we'll be hard-pressed to come up with something useful for them to do. That part of it might just be fun.

The saddest commentary of all is this: we may assume that the Christian Church, in particular the mainstream denominations, has been heavily infiltrated by these weasels, even in the traditional Bible Belt. Satan knows his enemy, even if we do not.

So we have a political party that supports homosexual activists, labor unions, including the extremely dangerous teachers' unions, the race baiters, feminists, Hollywood elite, and those old leftists who still cling feebly but enthusiastically to the Stalinist creed. They were fronted in this contest by "Moses" Lieberman, he of the elastic morals, and Al Gore, he of the no morals whatsoever. Admittedly, these wretches are worthy successors to Bill Clinton, and for those who believe as they believe, Lieberman and Gore are satisfactory if not inspiring. No soul-searching on the left, no honor or desire to do the best thing for the country. Just naked venality and an overwhelming lust for power. Even the more principled leftists abandoned them in disgust and went for Nader.

Essentially, this element of our body politic is at war with the principals upon which this country was founded and the people who believe in those principals. They want our money and they want our souls. They want absolute power, and they want it in the name of some bastardized imitation of democracy where everyone can have all the sex they want and call it freedom. It reeks of the barnyard – Orwell was strangely prescient in his use of metaphor.

It is time to consider that and forget this loyal opposition nonsense. Get it through your heads that these people are most definitely not loyal. There is no "agreeing to disagree" with this bunch, no compromise. Study the workings of the communist party from the thirties and forties and you will soon learn where the Democrats get this incredible tenacity – they will never stop: every compromise is to them, a short step forward toward their devilish goal of absolute power.

They will use whatever tactics it takes, and that includes importing millions of foreigners and declaring them citizens to skew the election results. They proved that by doing it: both in the recent election and in '96. At the rate they are flooding this country with immigrants, immigrants beholden to them, we can soon forget about western European culture. This benefits no one, not even the immigrants, and will lead to anarchy.

So I say to Mr. Puckett, and to the others out there who wish to work within the system, that the time for compromise was over years ago. Ask your kids what they are learning in school. I'm not just speaking to Southerners here. How about you Northern Californians who are virtually dominated by the leftists in your state? How about you westerners, who learned in this recent farce of an election that your voice is literally a voice crying in the wilderness. Clinton stole another eighty million acres of your land while the country was focused on the election! There are additionally, large blocks of freedom loving individuals in the northeast. What about them? Do you reckon they really like seeing homosexuals flood into Vermont to participate in the now "legal" mockery of God's own institution, marriage? How must it feel to live under the yoke of the socialist upstarts in Massachusetts or New York?

Can we roll over any longer? Immigration wasn't discussed in this election yet it is the second most crucial issue facing this country, with the exception of the slaughter of unborn children. The latter issue apparently doesn't exist on our political landscape either. Even those of you who disagree with me on that must admit that there has been no political or electoral dialogue on the issue: it was decided by the Supreme Court, the chief agency of our decline. Working well outside its constitutional authority I might add. Shouldn't issues like these be decided by the states?

In the midst of this upheaval, the government is quietly usurping our God-given right to own weapons of self-defense. We don't even need a constitution to see the logic in that one – if the government has the guns and we don't, the government owns us, and if you think that is too simplistic, then consider why the framers wrote so copiously about that very issue. Indeed, our constitution and Bill of Rights are designed for one purpose only: to limit government. How sickening it is to hear these tawdry politicians even mention the constitution they are sworn to uphold. Can we continue under the rule of such men? Dare we?

Mr. Puckett continues his argument by saying " all of the United States is ours." Well, it sure doesn't seem like it to me. If a cop in the Northern states pulls me over and finds my sidearm, I'm going to jail. If the government has its way, that despotism will soon find its way into the South as well. So no, let's not pretend all of these United States are ours. In New York, arguably one of the most dangerous towns in the US, we are required to walk around unarmed. Presumably, this is acceptable to New Yorkers or they would not tolerate it. Yet homosexuals dressed as nuns caper in the streets and no perversity is too vile to tolerate except the outmoded desire for political freedom. Do I wish to be ruled over by such people? Is it worth it? Let them have their way, but only with each other. And make them apply for visas to come here!

People on the left of the argument wish to tell us what to do, and are doing so. We are rolling over supinely and may well be fully cooked before we realize we're even in the oven. That these people are often well-meaning is of scant consequence to me. A dummy can hurt me just as easily as a wise, evil antagonist. That they will is obvious from the state of our education system, and from the systemic acceptance of the demise of our constitutional republic. For those slow learners out there, take a look at our penal system, and the police. Do constitutional republics lock up or shoot people for smoking a weed? To you Christian brothers let me add that the very police state being brought to bear in the drug war you have been supporting, will ultimately be used against you as well. Time to put on the thinking caps folks.

Perhaps this recent attempt at an electoral coup will alert people to the danger we face. And perhaps not... Stealing the votes of military men must certainly set a new standard for sheer venality yet where are the public cries of outrage. They may well get away with it.

I've actually heard people on the other side blaming the Republicans for trying to steal the election. As if the vacuous Republicans would have the gusto to fight dirty. What we learn from this, however, is that our country is irrevocably divided. They are not going to convince us, and we are not going to convince them. Despite the fact that many leftists are decent people trying to do the right thing, it's time to realize that their core beliefs are evil and to separate from them lest we be further corrupted by them.

Despite the traitor Clinton's efforts to subvert the military, that remains the single largest group in America that does not embrace his beastly ideas. Military personnel actually believe in the constitution, at a rate far exceeding that of say, public school teachers, politicians or TV news commentators. Will that military, most of whom are our neighbors, shoot us for exercising our constitutional right to separate? Probably not – but give the democrats another eight years and the military will be purged to the point where it will become the storm troopers of America and then we better watch out. They are rapidly weeding out the real soldiers and turning our military into an extension of the PC police.

Another eight years of these wretches and another generation will have been turned against us by the media and the public schools. We cannot afford to wait. We must raise up leaders among us who will take a stand and who will get us out of this tainted union with evil. We are out of time, we must do it now, and we must make it stick.

Here in America, the people who still believe in freedom have reached the point of no return. It can only go downhill for us from here. We must act, or we will have to learn to kiss the boot of an oppressor who is not only evil, but boring. That's right, I said boring. Hitler was charismatic in his evil – Stalin was downright demonic. Take a long hard look at Al Gore – his principals, if such a one can be said to have any, are very much in line with theirs. Yet this is a mediocre villain of a man who even while grasping rapaciously for power, provokes a yawn – a tedious despotism may well be the worst of all!

A final consideration for every Christian who contemplates secession must be this: we are enjoined by the very Word of God to respect the power of the state. I have considered this one at great length – to be found disobedient by the One who died that we might have life would be dreadful. So, we must consider the Office of the State, that second kingdom of God, the one which wields the sword. Our loyalty to the state is commanded of us in holy Scripture.

In America – we the people are the state, and we live in a constitutional republic which has been usurped. Ours is a voluntary union of states – an old and familiar argument, in no way obviated by the ruthless application of coercive force applied by the central government against us in 1861. We are indeed remiss, but only in that we have failed in our first duty which is to govern ourselves responsibly.

As a Lutheran, I believe more than most in separation of the church and state, and fear the possibility of a theocracy. I can't imagine why I'm not allowed to buy beer on Sunday yet conversely, neither can I imagine why on earth we tolerate leaders who would forbid us the guidance of the Ten Commandments in the courtroom! It has been noted that ours has become a country where the unborn are murdered in the womb yet the dead can vote and run for office. A country that sins corporately will be judged corporately and I have no wish to be judged for the sins of those who are currently running this country.

Since America was defined as a loose confederation of states, I'm convinced that we in no way violate the law of God as defined by Paul in Romans and by Peter in his epistles, when we espouse secession. Secession was and is, a natural and perfectly normal response of states which have become dissatisfied with the union into which they voluntarily entered. Remember that the legality of this was put to the test when the Yankees failed to try Jefferson Davis for treason because they could not find a law under which to prosecute him. Exercising the rights inherent in our form of government is in no way sedition!

It is our legal right (despite the war criminal Lincoln's admonitions to the contrary) to separate and separate we must.

The real question is this: why have let it go this far, that secession has become our last hope for an existence as free men?

Originally posted on lewrockwell.com, included in the collection of Secessionist Papers with the express consent and support of the author

Second Edition Commentary
By Barry Lee Clark

Mr. Peirce's contribution to this work represents a very specific time and place in the climate of American politics. One might presume from his words that he later went on to become an early Trump supporter in the 2016 election. Perhaps he did, perhaps not, but certainly many people that felt the frustrations, fears and concerns during and after the Clinton presidency Piece expressed in 2000 did, in fact, go on to become the corps of early and strong supporters of Donald Trump.

Liberals and conservatives both would be well served to read and re-read Peirce's words from 2000. The political environment in the United States is more divided in 2018 than at any time since 1861. (Pew, 2017) Real dialogue seldom occurs. Both sides increasingly feel disenfranchised by the views of the other. This appears to be trending toward greater misunderstanding, animosity and anger, on both sides.

Historically, this has proven to be an untenable and dangerous situation in other nations in the West. World War Two resulted primarily from a marked divide between two ideologies that could no longer coexist. If the trend of division, false narratives and anger continues apace in the United States it is not inconceivable to envision some future circumstance in which real violence occurs and one side truly over-powers the other, resulting in an abandonment of rationality (Tocqueville) and a tyranny of the majority.

Nobody, right or left, wants to suffer such a fate and no rational human wishes to see a circumstance where differences in ideology result in violence. I submit; however, this is the path we are treading.

Secession, devolution and a division of powers as originally envisioned and promised by the framers of the Constitution is a very real and practical solution to this pending problem.

Secessionist No. 8: Free Association

By Dr. Walter E. Block
July 9, 2002

The law of free association is a crucially important implication of the rights of private property (in physical material, and in our own bodies). For if we cannot freely associate with others on a mutually voluntary basis, our property rights are to that extent abrogated.

The most serious denigration of property rights in persons and thus in free association is, of course, murder. No one favors such behavior (killing in self-defense is entirely another matter) so this is not at all controversial. Another grave violation of the libertarian code of non-aggression against non-aggressors and their property is slavery (or kidnapping, which is short-term slavery). This, too, is non-debatable.

There are, however, many institutions, actually favored by "respectable" commentators on political economy, which partake of slavery to a greater or lesser extent. All laws against "discrimination" are violations of free association, because they force two parties, one of which who wishes to have nothing to do with the other, to interact despite these desires. When a store owner is forced to sell to customers against his will, and is not free to snub any of them on whatever racial, sexual, religious etc., basis he chooses, he is to that extent a slave. The difference between such laws and outright slavery is only one of degree: in each case, the essence of the matter is that people are forced to associate with others against their will. Another instance is forced unionism. Our labor legislation forces employers to "bargain fairly" with those they would prefer to avoid entirely.

Perhaps the most important violation of the law of free association, at least on pragmatic grounds, occurs in the political realm. This is crucial, because other infringements, such as affirmative action, union legislation, etc., stem from political sources. If freedom of association in the realm of affirmative action is the right to discriminate, and in the field of labor the right to hire a "scab," then when it comes to the political realm, it is the right to secession.

Those who are not free to secede are in effect (partial) slaves to a king, or to a tyrannous majority under democracy. Nor is secession to be confused with the mere right to emigrate, even when one is allowed to take one's property out of the country.

Secession means the right to stay put, on one's own property, and either to shift alliance to another political entity, or to set up shop as a sovereign on one's own account.

Why should the man who wishes to secede from a government have to vacate his land?

For surely, even under the philosophy of statists, it was the people who came first. Government, in the minarchist libertarian view, was only instituted by them in order to achieve certain ends, later, after they had come to own their property. That is to say, the state is a creation of the people, not the people a creation of the state. But if a government was once invited in, to provide certain services, then it can also be uninvited, or invited to leave, or expelled. To deny this is to assert that the government was there first, before there were even any people. But how can this be? Government is not a disembodied entity, composed of creatures other than human (although, perhaps, there may be legitimate doubts about this on the part of some); rather, it is comprised of flesh and blood, albeit for the most part evil, people.

Given, then, that secession is a human right, part and parcel of the right to free association, how can we characterize those who oppose this? Who would use force and violence, of all things, in order to compel unwilling participants to join in, or to remain part of, a political entity they wish to have nothing to do with? Why, as would be slave holders, of a sort. Certainly not as libertarians.

Thus, it is nothing short of amazing to find that there are commentators who actually call themselves libertarians and yet oppose the rights of secession. Were these people to remain consistent with this view, they would be logically forced, also, to give their imprimatur to union and anti-discrimination legislation, surely a *reductio ad absurdum*.

One of the grounds upon which so called libertarians oppose secession, the right to be left alone politically speaking, is that those who wish to secede might be less than fully perfect in various ways. For example, the Confederate states practiced slavery, and this is certainly incompatible with libertarian law.

Let us assume away the awkward historical fact that this "curious institution" was operational in the north, too. After all, we are making a philosophical point, not a historical one. Let us posit, *arguendo*, that the north came to its confrontation with the south with totally clean hands as far as slave holding, or, indeed, any other deviation from libertarian law is concerned (e.g., tariffs, high taxes, etc.). That is, the north is a totally libertarian entity, the south a morally evil one. (I know, I know; I'm only talking here for argument's sake).

Would that premise be a valid rationale for the north to in effect enslave the south, and thus violate its rights of free association? It would not.

If it was proper for the north to hold the south captive against its will, the implication is that India was not warranted in seceding from England in 1948 since the latter practiced suttee; that African countries were not justified in departing from their European colonial masters since they practiced clitorectemy; that it would not have been permissible for the Jews in 1930s Germany to have left the jurisdiction of the Nazis since they, too, were doubtless imperfect in some way or other.

Let us move from the realm of the macro to that of the micro. If groups of imperfect people are not justified in seceding from groups of perfect people, what about individuals? If we rigorously apply the principle on the basis of which confederate secession was opposed to the individual level, again we run into all sorts of counterintuitive results.

For example, divorce. Under this "logic" no spouse could leave another if the departing one were less than perfect.

In the words of Clyde Wilson: "If the right of secession of one part of a political community is subject to the moral approval of another, then there really is no right of secession." Either you have the right of free association and secession, or you do not.

If secession is always and everywhere justified, what, then, is the proper libertarian response to the existence of suttee, slavery, clitorectomy, etc., in other countries (e.g., in seceding territories)?

Under libertarian free market anarchism, it would be permissible for a private defense agency to invade private property if a crime is occurring there (if a mistake is made in this regard, libertarian punishment theory, the topic for another day, kicks into gear; in this type of society, even the police are not above the law). If A is about to murder B in A's house, A may not properly object when the police kick in his door to forestall this dastardly act. Thus, free market competing defense agencies could have gone into the south to free the slaves, but once this was done, given that there were no other crimes occurring, and that due punishment was meted out to the evil-doers, that would be the end of the matter. There would be no further interaction. The south (or India in the case of suttee) would then be allowed to go its own way.

Under limited government libertarianism, the government of the north would take no steps to rid the sovereign Confederacy of its slavery (or India of its suttee). The purpose of the state in this philosophy is to protect its own citizens. Period. And, on the (historically accurate) assumption that the Confederacy showed no indication of invading the north, but merely wanted to be left alone to its own devices, that would be the end of the matter as far as the northern government was concerned.

However, even under these assumptions individual abolitionists would be perfectly free, and, indeed, justified, in going in to the Confederacy, guns in hand, with the intention of ridding the south of this evil institution of slavery. But if things went poorly for them, they could not then scurry back to the north, tails between their legs, hiding behind their mama's skirts, because that would necessarily bring in the northern government into the fray. It would violate the non-invasion (except in self-defense) provision of limited government libertarianism, or minarchism.

There would be no "reconstruction." There would be no "indivisible" U.S.A. Rather, there would now be two totally separate countries. The U.S.A. and the Confederacy. Again, once slavery was ended, given that there were no other crimes occurring, and that due punishment was meted out to the evil-doers, that would be the end of the matter. On the (historically accurate) assumption that the Confederacy showed no indication of invading the north, but merely wanted to be left alone to its own devices, that would be the end of the matter as far as the northern government was concerned.

Included in the collection of Secessionist Papers with the express consent and support of the author.

Secessionist No. 9: Taking Secession Seriously, A Primer

by Hugh Williamson   August 3, 2001

Given the growing appreciation of the need for personal restraint and for institutional means for obtaining agreement amidst great social and political conflict, secession has become especially relevant to the present situation in the Western world – marked as it is by growing ethnic and cultural crises and social fragmentation. It is perhaps time to reconsider secession as a potential remedy – and as a return to the fundamentals of popular control.

The verb "secede" is derived from the Latin "*secedere*," meaning any act of withdrawal. Originally introduced in the seventeenth century as a concept of political theory, secession assumed the existence of the modern state, as well as the possibility of dismemberment of the state. In an American context, it has been misunderstood as simply the withdrawal by the Southern states from the Federal Union following the election of Abraham Lincoln to the presidency in November of 1860.

The structure of the political system, the original intentions of some framers of the constitution, and the citizenry's prevailing understanding of the political order during the Early encouraged a diversity of opinions regarding the fundamental nature of the union. Concerns arose in many quarters during the Constitutional Convention and ratification process, especially among the Antifederalists who feared that an overbearing national government would assume the authority of the states. Article Two of the Articles of Confederation had contained explicit provisions for protecting states, initiating a system whereby "each state retains its sovereignty." Various early state constitutions included provisions outlining the primacy of states in the confederal arrangement, often at the expense of a unified political order. The most popular form of amendment requested during the state ratification conventions and proposed to the First Congress concerned a reserved powers clause.

The defenders of the Constitution argued such a provision was unnecessary. James Madison suggested in Federalist 39 that each state was "a sovereign body" only "bound by its voluntary act" of ratification. Other Federalists, including James Wilson, Alexander Hamilton, and John Marshall at the Virginia ratifying convention, held that such a proposal was already present in the Constitution and that the new government would only have the powers delegated to it. Opposition to and suspicion of the proposed Constitution on the grounds that it would infringe upon the privileged status of the states was widespread.

On the other hand, the advocates of state authority viewed the states as the repository of reserved power, and many believed that states were invested with an equal, and perhaps superior capacity to judge infractions against the federal government. The most significant assurances to this effect came in the Virginia ratifying convention from George Nicholas and Edmund Randolph. As the spokesmen for the committee that reported the instrument of ratification, they noted that the Constitution would only have the powers "expressly" delegated to it. If Federalists disagreed with the stress on state authority, they generally viewed a reserved power clause as innocuous, and Madison included such a provision among the amendments he introduced in 1789.

In the First Congress, Elbridge Gerry, a founder and Antifederalist elected to the House of Representatives, introduced a proposal reminiscent of the Articles, leaving to the states all powers "not expressly delegated" to the federal government. Gerry's proposal was defeated, in part due to concerns about the similarity between the language of his amendment and the Articles. Others who took a states' rights or strict constructionist view of the Constitution, including Thomas Jefferson, persisted in defending state power. Before ratification of the Tenth Amendment, Jefferson advised President Washington that incorporating a national bank was unconstitutional. Jefferson would later compose the Kentucky Resolutions, which defended the states as the sovereign building blocks of the American nation and noted that the states retained a means of protection when threatened. To describe the process of state action Jefferson supplied a new term, nullification, to note the immediacy and severity of the "remedy" necessary to prohibit the federal government from absorbing state authority.

Defenders of the federal government, sometimes described as nationalists or loose constructionists, argued that the Congress must assume more power if the needs of the country were to be met. Most prominent among the advocates of increased federal authority was Alexander Hamilton. For Hamilton, the explicit protection of state prerogatives was unnecessary as the political order already protected states. The Constitution, according to the nationalists, also contained provisions for the exercise of federal power, including the "necessary and proper" and "supremacy" clauses.

The Supreme Court addressed the controversy in its McCulloch v. Maryland (1819) decision. The High Court upheld the constitutionality of a national bank, even though such an institution was not specified in the Constitution. In dismissing a strict delineation of state and federal authority, the Court under the leadership of John Marshall extended the powers of Congress at the expense of the states. On the other hand, the Marshall Court affirmed the excepted notion that police powers belonged exclusively to the states. Under Chief Roger Brooke Taney (1836-1854), the Court assumed more of a strict constructionist posture.

The emerging defense of state authority, and ultimately, was an interpretation of the American political experience, with an emphasis upon the original dispersion of authority, sovereignty, and restraint within the Constitution of 1787. According to understanding, offered by Calhoun and Hayne among others, the original system was predicated upon reserving the states' sphere of authority, while delegating sufficient authority for particular and limited responsibility to the general government. For Calhoun, this original diffusion, buttressed by a prudent mode of popular rule, was the primary achievement of American politics. A necessary corollary to his understanding of the regime's historical evolution was the need to perpetuate the original vision of the Union for posterity's sake: "The Union: Next to our liberty, the most dear; may we all remember that it can only be preserved by respecting the rights of the states and distributing equally the benefit and the burden of Union," urged Calhoun. If, as Calhoun suggested, America had "departed" from its "original character and structure," a recovery of the older design was necessary.

For the defenders of states' rights and secession, the Declaration of Independence initiated the legitimate delineation of state and federal authority and a properly constituted mode of popular rule through first articulating the primary nature of the union. According to this view that was shared by Southerners and most Americans, the Declaration illuminated and explained the foundations of the American republic as also resting upon a political compact. In contradistinction to a social compact, a political compact did not unite individuals or governments. Instead, such an agreement formed a republic with the same equality of rights among the States composing the Union, as among the citizens composing the States themselves.

The Declaration encouraged a political compact that had developed with "time and experience" into a model of political and social stability. The Declaration preserved the locus of authority within each individual state and allowed for secession when government "becomes destructive of these ends, it is the right of the people to alter or abolish it." For many Americans, the Declaration expressed the foundation for popular rule and a territorial republic that came to fruition in the Constitution. While the Declaration appropriately described the status of "Free and Independent States" as intrinsic to the republic, the document also confirmed the conceptual thesis of secessionist political theory: the states' "ordained" or created the republic.

If the Declaration supplied the prologue to the original design for the republic, it was the Articles of Confederation, the first American embodiment of the design, that incorporated this insight into the fundamental law of the regime. For Southerners, the provisions and language of the Articles served as an authentic precursor to the American Constitution. The Constitution of 1787 was incomprehensible without first assimilating the defense of states' rights contained in the Articles. Drafted in stages from 1776 to 1777, the Articles extended and revised the Declaration's ennobling of diffused authority and the delineation of state autonomy, while establishing popular rule based upon the deliberative, decentralized, community-centered participation of the citizenry. As in the case of the Declaration, the Articles perpetuated the original design for the territorial division of the country, into independent and sovereign States, on which the secessionist argument would later rest.

By strengthening the foundations laid by the Articles, the Constitution provided the final and most profound manifestation of the secessionist worldview's defense of popular rule and the diffusion of political authority. While the Declaration and Articles contributed to this evolving discernment, the Constitution presented the definitive maturation from a confederacy to a federal government, resting upon the authentic organic and delineatory manifestations of the states, although the citizenry retained final and complete political authority. Such a Constitution, in Calhoun's view, was most appropriately identified as a concurrent constitution because it served primarily as an exemplification of the states' role in preserving the regime. The Constitution also provided a careful "enumeration" and "specification" of power consigned to the general government. In other words, by forming a concurrent foundation for the political order it was argued that in times of crisis the states should exert their concurrent prerogative and repossess certain delegated power from the federal government if needed and in accord with the Constitution – especially in situations where the federal government had usurped power from the states. Through the adoption of the Constitution, the American people accepted a "joint supplemental government" that retained the states as the primary voice of the people.

In situations where the general government and the states were in conflict, each possessed a "mutual negative" on the other's actions, according to the secessionist argument. Defenders of secession often cited the record of the Virginia ratifying convention and the Tenth Amendment to the Constitution as primary evidence of the doctrine. The Virginia convention provided, along with its New York counterpart, the most erudite and complete commentary on the interpretation of the fundamental law besides the records of the Constitutional Convention itself. In situations of disputed authority, the states possessed the right of self-protection, with secession serving as the ultimate manifestation of such a response.

Struggles over the basis of the union arose after the ratification of the Constitution, including Jefferson's and Madison's response to President John Adams and the Alien and Sedition Acts of 1798. Defenders of state and national supremacy often changed positions depending of their political needs. In an effort to reduce the hardships incurred by the War of 1812, some New Englanders held a convention in Hartford, Connecticut, in 1814, as New England states were threatening secession. The first debate over secession in America took place in New England, not in the South.

The ensuing crises over Missouri statehood (1819-1820) and nullification (1832-1833) would increase secessionist tensions, but these problems would be resolved by compromise. The problem of slavery, compounded by the rise of abolitionism, would intensify the conflict. After Southerners were able to defeat the Wilmot Proviso, the Compromise of 1850 made resolution of the slavery problem more problematic. In 1854, Senator Stephen A. Douglas of Illinois, attempting to garner support from southern congressman for his legislation that would organize the territories of Kansas and Nebraska, reopened the issue of extending slavery into new areas. The passage of the Kansas-Nebraska Act unified resistance to slavery in the North, and by 1854 the Republican Party was dominant in the region. The election of James Buchanan to the presidency in 1856 and the constitutionally sound, but unpopular ruling of the Supreme Court in the Dred Scott case in 1857, widened the sectional divide.

Lincoln's election in 1860 galvanized Southern attitudes in favor of secession. In Lincoln, the South correctly feared its established way of life and fundamental rights would be threatened. The success of a minority political party, the Republicans, in electing a president was a source of some disdain as well. Agitated by the advocates of secession known as "fire-eaters," and the failure of other efforts to ameliorate the tension, South Carolina withdrew from the Union, having passed a secession ordinance on December 20, 1860; South Carolina was followed in quick succession by Mississippi, Florida, Alabama, Georgia, Louisiana, and Texas. After the incident at Fort Sumter in April 1861, and Lincoln's call for troops, Virginia, Arkansas, Tennessee, and North Carolina adopted secession ordinances and eventually joined the Confederacy.

The remainder of the story, including the War of Northern Aggression, is much more familiar. Unfortunately, the fable of secession's demise as an authentic element in the American political and constitutional tradition is still preached with great vigor. The related and prevailing notion that the Supreme Court's Texas v. White decision (1869), and its defense of the "perpetuity and indissolubility of the Union," closed the debate over secession distracts the country from the enduring importance of the concept. In the decision itself, Chief Justice Salmon P. Chase conceded that the citizenry maintained a right of revolution and that the role of the people in exercising their constitutional right should not be diminished.

As we ponder the necessity of revitalizing the role of states and – especially their interposing and amending power so implicit in the Constitution – we could only augment authentic popular rule by allowing for a greater diffusion of authority. The critics of secession have argued that restricting the ability of the general government to act might in some fashion produce its own variety of hegemonic or tyrannical rule. Unfortunately, these assessments misrepresent secession as a political concept destined to undermine the structure of the American regime. In actuality, secession may actually allow for the preservation of the original balance of authority and the fortification of a political system against the obstacles it faces. The vindication of a Southern defense of diffused authority can be witnessed in the negative effects of the centralization of political power in America and the world throughout this century.

- Adams, Charles. When in the Course of Human Events: Arguing the Case for Southern Secession. Lanham, Maryland: Rowman and Littlefield, 2000.
- Berger, Raoul. Federalism: The Founders' Design. Norman: University of Oklahoma Press, 1987.
- Buchanan, Allen. Secession. Boulder, Colorado: Westview Press, 1991.
- Calhoun, John C. A Discourse on the Constitution and Government of the United States, in Union and Liberty: The Political Philosophy of John C. Calhoun. Edited by Ross M. Lence. Indianapolis: Liberty Fund, 1992.
- Cheek, H. Lee. Calhoun and Popular Rule. Columbia, Missouri: University of Missouri Press, 2001.
- The Documentary History of the Ratification of the Constitution, Volumes VIII-X: Ratification of the Constitution by the States, Virginia. Edited by John P. Kaminski, Gaspare J. Saladino, et al. Madison, Wisconsin: State Historical Society of Wisconsin, 1993.
- Freehling, William W. The Road to Disunion: Secessionists at Bay, 1776-1854. New York: Oxford University Press, 1990.

• Gordon, David, Editor. Secession, State and Liberty.
New Brunswick, New Jersey: Transaction Publishers,
1998.

Secessionist No. 10: Secede!

by Dr. Thomas E. Woods, Jr. August 11, 2000
Secession, State and Liberty Edited with an introduction
by David Gordon New Brunswick, NJ: Transaction, 1998,
344pp.

On a daily basis we are confidently assured by the
organs of respectable opinion that the process of
globalization is continuing smoothly, the old-fashioned
conception of national sovereignty gradually giving way
to the idea of supranational governance. Yet this
confident note is not without a certain dissonance, for at
the very moment when a New World Order is supposed
to be emerging, the world finds itself confronted as
never before by movements for secession, devolution,
and local control. Professor Donald Livingston has
observed that no more than twenty-five-member states
of the United Nations can claim to be free of such
conflicts.

Secession in its historical and philosophical aspects is
the topic of an outstanding volume of papers first
delivered several years ago at a conference on the
subject sponsored by the Ludwig von Mises Institute in
Auburn, Alabama. Entitled Secession, State, and Liberty,
the collection is edited with an introduction by David
Gordon, a brilliant intellectual historian about whom it
has more than once been said, "Who needs the Library
of Congress when you have David Gordon?" The result is
an extraordinarily compelling work of scholarship
bristling with insight and little-known facts.

The idea of secession, although associated in the popular mind with radicalism and – inanely – even treason since the Southern states attempted to withdraw from the Union during the 1860s, was a common one during the first several generations of the republic's existence. Tom DiLorenzo's essay on the subject sheds important historical light on what has been anything but a merely theoretical question throughout American history. In each case DiLorenzo examines – from rumblings following the Louisiana Purchase through the War of 1812 – the matter in dispute was the wisdom and prudence of a given state's withdrawal from the Union at a particular time; that the states had the right to withdraw was simply taken for granted.

None of this would have startled Thomas Jefferson. Jefferson refused to view the American Union as anything more than a utilitarian political arrangement to be judged by the test of time, and he expected it ultimately to devolve into two or three independent confederacies – a development he did not view with any particular dread. He told James Madison that he was "determined...to sever ourselves from the union we so much value rather than give up the rights of self-government...in which alone we see liberty, safety and happiness." When Daniel Webster attempted to argue against the principled states' rights position in famous debates with Robert Hayne and John C. Calhoun during the 1830s, the best assurance he could offer them against the possibility of federal tyranny was the check provided by popular elections – an alleged safeguard to which the verdict of history has not been kind.

In an excellent essay on "Republicanism, Federalism, and Secession in the South, 1790-1865," Mises Institute Historian in Residence Joseph Stromberg discusses the origins of secessionist theory and, among many other examples, looks to the case of the Virginia and Kentucky Resolutions of 1798. Madison and Jefferson, respectively, penned these resolves in response to the recently passed and constitutionally dubious Alien and Sedition Acts. Jefferson's, not surprisingly, was the more radical of the two, insisting on a state's right to "nullify" laws it considered unconstitutional; this, Jefferson insisted, was the only way to ensure that the general government would not come to oppress the states by construing the Constitution however it pleased. Liberal historians, Stromberg notes, argue disingenuously that the resolutions were part of a battle over freedom of expression only; in fact, they were the battleground of a struggle for states' rights that would be a perennial theme throughout American history.

Picking up Jefferson's line of argument several decades later, John C. Calhoun, in his own defense of nullification, insisted again and again that if the federal government were allowed to determine the extent of its own powers, no mere piece of paper, however venerable, could stop it. The states had to be able to assert their sovereignty in a serious and forceful way if the federal compact were to retain its integrity as a joint agreement between equals and not to degenerate into the consolidated tyranny that the framers feared.

For American readers the most compelling essay may be that of Donald Livingston, a world-renowned David Hume scholar and professor of philosophy at Emory University. Livingston demonstrates that the theory of the Union held by supporters of secession is grounded so much more firmly in American history than that of its opponents as to be almost laughable. To argue, as foes of secession must, that the United States was formed by the American people in the aggregate rather than by the sovereign capacity of preexisting states is to leave the terrain of serious historical argument and descend into a vapid mythology.

Livingston also reminds his readers of the overwhelming weight of the testimony of key American thinkers in favor of the principle that a state may freely withdraw from that Union into which it had freely entered. Thus he makes note of the important 1825 book by John Rawle, A View of the Constitution, which was so widely respected that it was used as a textbook at West Point from 1825-1840. Rawle, no friend of secession, conceded that under certain conditions it would be perfectly legal for a state to withdraw unilaterally from the federal compact. President-turned-congressman John Quincy Adams, another friend of union (albeit one who himself suggested the possibility of Northern secession over the issue of Texas annexation), observed in commemoration of the Constitution's fifty-year jubilee:

"The indissoluble link of union between the people of the several states of this confederated nation is, after all, not in the right but in the heart. If the day should ever come (may Heaven avert it!) when the affections of the people of these States shall be alienated from each other; when the fraternal spirit shall give way to cold indifference, or collision of interests shall fester into hatred, the bands of political associations will not long hold together parties no longer attracted by the magnetism of conciliated interests and kindly sympathies; and far better will it be for the people of the disunited states to part in friendship from each other, than to be held together by constraint."

Alexis de Tocqueville, moreover, the great French observer of American affairs, himself wrote that the Union *"was formed by the voluntary agreement of the states; and these, in uniting together, have not forfeited their nationality, nor have they been reduced the condition of one and the same people. If one of the states chose to withdraw its name from the contract, it would be difficult to disprove its right to do so."*

Clyde N. Wilson, editor of The Papers of John C. Calhoun and professor of history at the University of South Carolina, addresses the obvious objection that the states themselves are hardly bastions of liberty and culture these days. *"I know there are many moral and social problems that are not solved by political arrangements, and that the level of statesmanship in the states is not much higher, if at all, than in the federal government,"* he observes. *"But if we are to speak of curbing the central power, the states are what we have got. They exist. They are historical, political, cultural realities, the indestructible bottom line of the American system."*

This is precisely the point. Any effort to recover the old American republic must begin with its constituent parts, the states. And any serious thought on the subject must come to grips with the intellectually rigorous contributions – ranging in subject matter from the political theory of secession to analyses of devolutionist rumblings in Quebec and in Europe – to Secession, State and Liberty, a unique scholarly volume on a subject rarely accorded serious academic treatment. As Professor Wilson puts it, "It would be a shame if, in this world-historical time of devolution, Americans did not look back to an ancient and honorable tradition that lies readily at hand."

Thomas E. Woods, Jr., a 1994 graduate of Harvard College, holds a Ph.D. in history from Columbia University and is currently a professor of history at Suffolk Community College in Brentwood, New York.

The Secession Solution: A data-based plea for the Independent States of America

by Kirkpatrick Sale   from Chronicles January-February 2011

Aristotle declared that there should be a limit to the size of states. But really, what did he know? He lived at a time when the entire population of the world was somewhere around 50 million—about the size of England today. Athens, where he lived, would have been under 100,000 people. He couldn't even imagine a world (ours) of 6.8 billion, or a city (Tokyo) of 36 million. How is he going to help us?

He, at least, knew this much:

"Experience shows that a very populous city can rarely, if ever, be well governed; since all cities which have a reputation for good government have a limit of population. We may argue on grounds of reason, and the same result will follow: for law is order, and good law is good order; but a very great multitude cannot be orderly."

So political units, Aristotle said, have to be limited. And it is with that understanding that we now may start contemplating what in today's world would constitute the ideal, or optimum, size of a political state.

This is not some sort of idle philosopher's quest but the foundation of a serious reordering of our political landscape, and a reordering such as the process of secession— indeed, only the process of secession—could provide. The U.S. provides abundant evidence that a state as large as 310 million people is ungovernable. One scholar recently said that we are in the fourth decade of the U.S. Congress' inability to pass a single measure of social consequence. Bloated and corrupted beyond its ability to address any of the problems it has created as an empire, it is a blatant failure. So, what could replace it, and at what size? The answer is the independent states of America.

Let us start by looking at modern nations to give us some clue as to population sizes that actually work.

Among the nations that are recognized models of statecraft, eight are below 500,000— Luxembourg, Malta, Iceland, Barbados, Andorra, Liechtenstein, Monaco, and San Marino.

Of the 14 states generally reckoned freest in the world, 9 have populations below Switzerland's, at 7.7 million, and 11 below Sweden's, at 9.3 million; the only sizable states are Canada, the United Kingdom, and Germany (the largest, at 81 million). There are other national rankings. Literacy: Of the 46 countries that claim a literacy rate of 99 or better, 25 are below 7.5 million. Health: Measured by the World Health Organization, 9 of the top 20 are under 7 million. In 2009 rankings of happiness and standard of living, the top countries were Norway, Iceland, Sweden, Netherlands, Australia, Luxembourg, Switzerland, Canada, Ireland, Denmark, Austria, and Finland; all but Canada and Australia have small populations.

Enough of that. The point, I trust, is well and simply made. The figures seem to suggest that there is an optimum size of a successful state, somewhere in the range of 3 million to 5 million people.

Surprisingly, a great many countries are also modest in geographic terms—underlining the point, often missed by critics of secession, that a nation does not have to be self-sufficient to operate well in the modern world. In fact, there are 85 countries out of the 195 counted by the United Nations that are under 10,000 square miles—that is to say, the size of Vermont or smaller.

And if we measure economic strength by per capita GDP, small countries prove to be decidedly advantageous. Seventy-seven percent of the most prosperous countries are small. And most of them are quite small indeed: under 10,000 square miles.

Administrative, distribution, transportation, and similar transaction costs obviously rise, perhaps exponentially, as geographic size increases. Control and communication also become more difficult to manage over long distances, often to the point where central authority and governance become nearly impossible.

I propose that, out of these figures and even more so out of the history of the world, results a Law of Government Size, and it goes like this: Economic and social misery increase in direct proportion to the size and power of the central government of a nation.

The consolidation of nations into powerful empires leads not to shining periods of peace and prosperity and the advance of human betterment, but to increasing restriction, warfare, autocracy, crowding, immiseration, inequality, poverty, and starvation.
Small, then, is not only beautiful but also bountiful.
How does all of this apply to the United States today?

Of the 50 states, 29 have populations below 5 million people. Eight states and a colony in the 3 million to 5 million population class would be ideal secession candidates: Iowa, Connecticut, Oklahoma, Oregon, Puerto Rico, Kentucky, Louisiana, South Carolina, and

Alabama. Twelve—Rhode Island, Hawaii, New Hampshire, Maine, Idaho, Nebraska, West Virginia, New Mexico, Nevada, Utah, Kansas, and Arkansas—have between 1 million and 3 million people, and seven, including Vermont, have fewer than 1 million people but more than Iceland.

The argument for secession need not focus exclusively on population or geographic size—one might factor in cultural cohesion, developed infrastructure, historical identity—but that seems to be the sensible place to start in considering viable states. And since the experience of the world has shown that populations ranging from 3 million to 5 million are optimal for governance and efficiency, that is as good a measure as any to use to begin assessing secessionist potential and chances of success as independent states.

The only hope for reenergizing American politics is to create truly sovereign states through peaceful, popular, powerful secession.
Kirkpatrick Sale is director of the Middlebury Institute and the author of Human Scale.

Excerpted from Chronicles: A Magazine of American Culture (Oct.2010). **www.chroniclesmagazine.org**

Secessionist No. 11: A Biblical Defense of Localism

by Kevin L. Clauson

Secession is a process whereby one or more political entities remove themselves from the jurisdiction of another political entity (usually larger or more encompassing). It has been a hotly debated subject in theory in America ever since the Confederate States of America tried it in practice (and were defeated militarily). Most Americans do not realize that secession was threatened on at least two previous significant occasions, one of which involved the threatened secession of the New England States.

Is secession a legal-political remedy that is warranted by Scripture as a means of protecting "localism" (in America we sometimes call this "states' rights")? This article will answer this question, and in so doing take a biblical, theological, historical, and constitutional look at an issue which might someday face America (as it has diverse nations such as Canada, Nigeria, and the old Soviet Union).

We begin by turning to an often-neglected historical account from the Bible in 1 Kings 12:1-24. King Solomon had just died. Rehoboam, one of Solomon's sons, became the new king of all Israel. Jeroboam, a very astute and high official in Solomon's regime who had fled to Egypt because of an attempted rebellion, returned after the news of Solomon's death. Jeroboam and an apparently large contingent of leaders in Israel came to the new king, saying:

"Thy father made our yoke grievous: now therefore make thou the grievous service of thy father, and his heavy yoke which he put upon us, lighter, and we will serve thee." (1 Kings 12:4)

Jeroboam represented a large portion of the people in Israel who apparently had experienced some degree of tyranny or oppression during the latter years of Solomon's regime. (There is ample evidence from preceding chapters to indicate that Solomon had succumbed to idolatry, lost some control of his kingdom, and allowed others to exert oppressive control over the people, doing during the latter years of his regime many of the things foretold by God through Samuel in 1 Samuel 8.) He was petitioning the new regime to reduce this oppression--to exercise godly and righteous rule.

The passage continues by describing how Rehoboam promised an answer in three days and consulted both the "old men that stood before Solomon" (the old advisors and officials who wisely offered counsel that the king should lift the "heavy yoke" and he would have peace and loyalty--"If thou wilt be a servant unto this people this day, and wilt serve them...." 1 Kings 12:7) and the "young men that were grown up with him" (his young, inexperienced peers, who, as is customary with those who would ingratiate themselves with a ruler, told him what he probably wanted to hear, namely, that he should increase the oppression--"My little finger shall be thicker than my father's loins...and I will add to your yoke...." 1 Kings 12:10-11). Rehoboam followed the advice of the "young men." The people who were with Jeroboam answered this response: "What portion have we in David?" (1 Kings 12:16) Furthermore: "...when Israel heard that Jeroboam was come again, that they sent and called him unto the congregation and made him king over all Israel... [except] Judah." (1 Kings 12:20) Rehoboam prepares to fight Jeroboam; but the Lord directly intervenes to prevent this, saying, "for this thing is from me." (1 Kings 12:24)

What we see here is a rebellion of the "northern tribes" which takes the form of what we would call secession. While it is true that all of this took place to fulfill God's prophecy that the kingdom would be divided, which was a judgment upon Solomon for his evil (see 1 Kings 11:1-13 and 26-43, 1 Kings 12:15 and 1 Kings 12:24), nevertheless, there are also clear normative lessons regarding a "just revolution" generally and the more specific method of "just revolution" called secession or secessionism. What are the theological lessons from this historical incident?

Israel was a nation founded upon a very explicit covenant with God. Such a covenant involved a condition --the condition that the people and especially the rulers obey God's commandments. Under Rehoboam, this covenantal condition was broken. The civil authorities, that stood in a representative relationship to those who to one degree or another desired to retain or re-establish the covenant, after having sought redress of grievances through the proper procedural means, understood that Rehoboam was determined to break the civil covenant. Therefore, Jeroboam, in essence, purposed with the people of the "northern tribes" to re-establish the civil covenant in the "new" kingdom--Israel. To put it another way, Jeroboam and the northern tribes were continuing the covenant which all Israel was bound by, but which the current king Rehoboam broke. "Israel" then was simply a continuation of Israel in covenantal terms.

Where the cause is just (upholding the civil covenant), where all legal/peaceful means have been exhausted and rejected (petitions no longer matter), and where another civil authority or jurisdiction is legitimately leading the way in the just cause, then the basic conditions for a "just revolution" are present. This was so in the 1 Kings 12 account even though Jeroboam fairly quickly led his nation into corporate sin in setting up the golden calves for worship so that his people would not go to Jerusalem to worship and potentially be enticed back into the political orbit of Judah. The form that the just revolution took here, instead of the "capture" of the entire existing nation, was the seceding of a portion or remnant of the nation to create a new jurisdiction, free from the anti-covenantal unrighteous government of the original nation.

Such was the case, I would argue, in the American "War Between the States," 1861-1865. The national government, under the leadership of the Republican Party (which was at least partially influenced by "radical abolitionists") and Abraham Lincoln, had already broken or was in the process of breaking what the South perceived to be an existing civil covenant (embodied in a constitution). The Confederate States of America believed they were bringing continuity to this civil covenant whereas the national government was destroying it.[7] The agents of the "revolution" were state governments, legitimate civil jurisdictions in their own right. By the time Fort Sumter was fired upon all legal/peaceful means of remedy were already non-existent. (Lincoln was raising an army to attack the already-seceded states!)

Slavery was not the central issue, although like the "new" Israel under Jeroboam in its newly-created idolatrous worship of the golden calves, slavery may be considered an ancillary sin for which partial judgment was due. But note well that the argument against slavery, if it is to be legitimate, cannot be based on the crime of man-stealing, since manstealing had ceased and all that was left after many years was a system of slavery from which there was no ideally satisfactory escape. Many blacks were already free men, a much larger number were slaves, but as they were cared for by "owners" they possessed no strong feelings of leaving a life they had always known for a life of great uncertainty and potential hardship.

I say this not to dismiss the problem of slavery, but to put the whole situation in perspective; slavery (and many other matters) was plainly and clearly and totally under the jurisdiction of the states. For the national government to seriously talk of interfering with the states on the slavery issue was an assault on state sovereignty and the Constitution as Southerners had always understood it (a modified Articles of Confederation, no matter that it was less than perfect).

I would furthermore strengthen the case for secessionism (although I Kings 12 is enough) by pointing out a particular part of the U.S. Constitution which is almost unanimously interpreted today as being anti-secessionist, Article VI, section 2, the so called "Supremacy clause." This clause states:

This Constitution, and all laws of the United States which shall be made in pursuance thereof...shall be the supreme law of the land; and the judges in every state shall be bound thereby, anything in the Constitution or laws of any state to the contrary notwithstanding.

Far from meaning that whatever Congress legislates is automatically the "supreme law of the land" which the states are bound to uphold, this clause clearly means that only those federal laws which are pursuant to the Constitution are the supreme law, and if such laws are not pursuant to the Constitution, they are not the supreme law of the land and do not have to be upheld by the states. This in turn implies strongly that the states (i.e. state governments) have a duty to interpret the U.S. Constitution just as much as any federal branch of government.

This itself is nothing new but is a doctrine affirmed by John Calvin in Book IV of The Institutes of the Christian Religion, where he writes of the power of the "lesser magistrate" to use interposition, i.e., to interpose or stand between the people under his jurisdiction and some larger civil government, to stop the evil or tyranny of that larger government. [59]

I would argue that Article VI, section 2 of the U.S. Constitution allows, indeed requires, the same of the states vis-a-vis the national government where the national government is attempting to impose (and to use the states to help impose) some unconstitutional evil. Secession is simply a higher more advanced stage of the concept of interposition (or "nullification," or in simple terms, disobedience). It is an ultimate form of "just revolution" by another civil jurisdiction. It involves the removal of a political "subdivision" from the jurisdiction of the larger entity where the larger entity has "broken covenant." (It should be added that if there is really no righteous civil covenant, then a seceding jurisdiction is really doing nothing more than forming a new tyranny-- an attempt to create a "big fish in a smaller pond"-- unless the seceding entity is establishing a heretofore non-existent godly covenant.)

In modern times, the most astounding example of secession was that of the former soviet republics (such as Ukraine, Armenia, Latvia, etc.) from the old Union of Soviet Socialist Republics. Whether all of the seceding republics left in order to perpetuate a more biblical civil covenant is highly doubtful. Nevertheless, this secession certainly caused the collapse of the former "evil empire," an event about which God is surely pleased since He brought it about. It is exceedingly difficult for any modern observer to celebrate the collapse of the Soviet Union and simultaneously decry Southern secession and secessionism in general. This is all the truer when one considers that while the soviet republics' secessions were motivated by a desire to be free from centralized tyranny (only in some cases to establish a decentralized tyranny), Southern secession was motivated by a desire to continue a civil covenant which was largely Christian. [60]

This is a similar case to the secession of the northern tribes from Israel (leaving only Judah) to create a "new" Israelite nation-state which was at least at first a more perfect continuation of the old Israel (until the "golden calves"). And I have argued that the division of Israel after the death of Solomon is a model-by-way-of-historical-illustration of all proper secessions.

The conclusion of the matter is that secession is a biblical, covenantal, constitutional mechanism for the protection and preservation of "states' rights." In the context of a Christian socio-political culture it is a mechanism which allows a new political entity to perpetuate the continuity of an older civil covenant which the original larger nation-state has broken. As such, it is a remedy we should never use lightly but always esteem highly. Let those who would preach union-at-any-cost (in perpetuity) prove otherwise.

A biblically-based analogy which comes to mind in support of the concept of secession is that of marriage. Marriage is a covenantal relationship under God. However, God has not said that the marriage bond must be maintained under all circumstances. If one party breaks the covenant, then it is annulled and a divorce (a secession from the marriage union) is justified (due to adultery, for example). It is folly for a pastor or elder to counsel an innocent woman whose husband has clearly and flagrantly committed adultery that she must remain married and that any divorce on her part is sin (for which she should "feel" guilt).

Likewise, it is folly to counsel a legitimate political entity (e.g., a state) that no matter how much its sovereignty is trampled upon it must remain perpetually in "the union," that no matter how much the larger government breaks the civil covenant the state must go along. (This is as bad as a local church knowingly remaining within a denomination which has clearly become a "Synagogue of Satan" for the sake of peace and unity.) Let not secession be used lightly and for transient reasons. But where called for, as Patrick Henry said: "Give me liberty or give me death." [61]

Kevin L. Clauson B.A. (International Relations), B.S. (Chemistry), M.A. (Political Science), Marshall University; J.D. (Law), West Virginia University. President, Christ College; President, The Patrick Henry Institute; Former Chair, Government Department, Liberty University; Professor of Government, Helms School of Government, Liberty University; Former Assistant Professor of Political Science, Grove City College. Married (since 1982); four children.

Secessionist No. 12: Small is Powerful

By Kirkpatrick Sale of the Middlebury Institute
Originally posted September 2005 on VT Commons

When you have a bunch of crushed grapes and introduce yeast cells, you produce one of the most energetic and successful events in biology. The yeast eats up the sugar of the grape and produces alcohol as a waste byproduct, and keeps on eating and eating, happy as a, well, yeast in juice—until there is no more sugar to eat, or the alcohol content gets close to 14 percent, at which point the yeast can no longer survive. It chokes, more or less, in its own waste. And the wine is made.

This is a process ecologists call drawdown. The next steps are bloom, crash, diedown, and dieout. That is the process of many species. It is the process through which industrial civilization is going today—only we are still in the first two phases of it. Drawdown of the world's resources at an alarming rate—to the point where the distinguished Harvard biologist E.O. Wilson has declared that "Earth's capacity to support our species is approaching the limit." Bloom, though of course not for everyone, but about a fifth of the world's population, and at levels of grandeur never before known to the earth.

But it is obvious that the other three ecological stages are upon us. We can already see that crash is coming. Wilson again: "The appropriation of productive land—the ecological footprint—is already too large for the planet to sustain" and "has stressed the earth beyond its ability to regenerate." That means that unless we drastically change our ways, soon, our species—the one that calls itself sapient—will crash and die down and possibly even die out, taking with us a great many other species on the surface of the earth.

It's very simple. There really is no argument about it. Not among serious people.

That's the problem. So, what's the solution? Also simple: localism.

Now there are many ways of going about that, and one of the great strengths of localism is that it takes different forms in different places, adapted to its context. But there are two forms that I think hold some real promise for the future: bioregionalism and separatism.

I won't bore you with a lot of stuff about bioregionalism—I've written a book, still available, that spells it out in some detail. For all its 7-syllable grandeur, it just means life-place, the way that nature has patterned herself, the scale at which she has organized distinctive flora and fauna, water and climate, rocks and soils. The borders of such bioregions of course are fuzzy, but they are there: the world, the continents, are really made up of small self-defining regions.

As original people everywhere knew. Like American Indians. I have seen a map of Indian tribes' territories in the mid-19th century, when the American government was trying to draw up treaties with them. Almost all the territories are watersheds of large rivers—in other words, bioregions that contain distinctive flora and fauna. That is the way the Indians naturally settled themselves, how they lived on the land.

As earth scientists know. The latest map from the U.S. Forest Service's Ecosystem Management Division in Fort Collins, Colorado, is of "Ecoregions of North America," with provinces mapped out by what can only be called a bioregional method, though naturally with an emphasis on trees because that's their charge. The result is essentially a map of bioregions.

As other professionals know. Geographers as long ago as 1985 began using the term; landscape architects, too, who were recently enjoined by the president of the American Society of Landscape Architects to operate with a "bioregional hypothesis."

As we all know, really, in our heart of hearts, when we stop to think of it. We know that we live in a natural region of some sort, with distinctive natural elements, a river, say, or a lake, or a mountain range. City dwellers tend to overlook this, and cities tend these days to ignore their hinterlands and look to the world. But most other people do see themselves as part of a region of some kind. They know where their water comes from and where it goes, what the typical animal and tree species are, and so on. Industrial capitalism has done much to destroy that identity, and globalism finds it anathema, but it is there nonetheless.

So bioregions are a reality, and bioregionalism is about trying to think about living, and growing and eating and traveling and using and eventually governing, within them. To put it briefly, the whole concept is simply trying to give people a new way of thinking about nature, and then acting within it.

That is the first, and the absolute necessary, principle by which we can think about localism. The other principle is separatism, which I take to encompass secession, regionalism, tribalism, self-determination, and all forms of devolution. It is clearly a movement of our time, whatever counterforces of globalism and imperialism exist. It is, as I've noted before, the worldwide trend since World War II, capped most recently by the break-up of Yugoslavia and the Soviet Union. It is also a strong and growing trend in the United States, for all the superficial unity wrought by mass marketing and mass media. The red-state and blue-state divisions are only one form of it, though they point to a real and serious gulf in the land.

The response to the last presidential election in this country has been regional and holds the seeds of a real separatist movement. A group on the West Coast called MoveonCalifornia was established in November 2004 and has since been holding meetings under the rubric of a "Committee to Explore California Secession." The League of the South, which has been pressing for Southern secession for some decades, has found renewed fervor for its cause. A group in New Mexico has proposed a "*Republica del Norte*" that might include Arizona, New Mexico, Texas, and southern Colorado.

Hawaii has three secessionist organizations and there's a move to have a statewide referendum on a return to the independent state it once was. The Alaska Independence Party has been a real force in the state for years—it even got Walter Hickel elected governor on its slate in 1991, though he soon rejected the party—and now has grown to more than 20,000 members, the largest statewide third party in America. And a group in New York City, connected to a weekly called the Brooklyn Rail, has been writing and meeting and propagandizing for a Free NYC movement.

It's too soon to say what any of these organizations will achieve. But it's important to see that they exist and they express a very deep-seated attitude of regionalism in this country that goes way back and has recently been revivified.

At one time our diets, sex lives, family relations, education, and jobs were all under the serious and daily control of churches and kings. We are no longer under their thrall, at least not in this country. Is it so fantastic to think about being as free of the regular interference of the government of the nation-state?

Let us think back to the emergence of the mammalian class, long eons ago. Their success was due to the fact that, unlike the dinosaurs that until then had dominated the earth, they were small and able to adapt to all kinds of diurnal and climatic conditions the big lizards were not. They were able to survive and eventually to proliferate, even dominate. Let us imagine we are in another political Eocene epoch now, again watching the emergence of nimble, smaller forms to challenge the old, collapsing dinosaurs of nation and empire.

Kirkpatrick Sale - is the author of numerous books, including *Human Scale* and *Dwellers in the Land: The Bioregional Vision* (University of Georgia Press). He is a founder and director of The Middlebury Institute for "the study of separatism, secession, and self-determination."

Secessionist No. 13: The Case for American Secession

By Kirkpatrick Sale of the Middlebury Institute
(Chronicles magazine, November 2005)

There has always been talk about secession in this country by those variously disgruntled on both the right and left, but since the last Presidential election, which showed great and deep-seated divisions in American society on a variety of fundamental issues, that talk has grown exponentially. I would not argue that it will actually lead to a dissolution of this nation into separate states or regions or confederacies, but that is not by any means inconceivable, and I would say that the issue should be taken seriously and examined carefully.

The first question to be asked, and it is not a frivolous one, is whether secession is legal—whether the Constitution can be read, and history cited, as permitting (or at least not forbidding) a state to declare its independence from the Union. Scholars have come down on both sides of this issue, but that fact alone suggests that there is a legitimate argument to be made. To put it simply:

The Tenth Amendment reserves powers not delegated to the U.S. to the states or the people, so states may act unless specifically prohibited. The Constitution in fact says nothing about secession, and as Confederate states were seceding Congress considered an amendment forbidding secession, which means that the principle wasn't there in the first place. Three of the original thirteen states (Rhode Island, New York, and Virginia) kept an explicit right to secede when they joined the Union, and since that was never challenged of questioned it must be a right that all states enjoy. And in the 19th century, before South Carolina began the bandwagon of secession in 1860, seven states (Kentucky, Pennsylvania, Georgia, South Carolina, Wisconsin, Massachusetts, and Vermont) enacted acts of nullification—meaning their refusal to recognize some or all of the powers of the national government—without any retaliation by Washington.

Of course, Lincoln's government acted as if secession were illegal and unconstitutional, and its victory established the practical case, operable to this day, that states will be punished if they try to secede, and the Constitution is irrelevant. But it did not establish a legal case, and the legal (not to mention moral) argument for the right to secede remains strong. So strong that even if it were denied in the U.S. courts it would likely be defended in the court of world opinion by many of the world's nations, including those in the European Union and those that have recently exerted that right (in the former Soviet Union and former Yugoslavia, for example). And that might make it difficult for the Federal government to act against a state that has voted for secession, particularly if there were no overriding moral issues (a la slavery) and the state proved agreeable to negotiation over Federal property and assets within its boundaries.

Even accepting that, a second question arises over whether a Federal government could allow a state or especially a group of states to secede, regardless of rights, if it threatened the sovereignty and power of the remaining nation. Washington might not want to let California go, as much as the neocons might like it, for fear that Cascadia (Oregon and Washington) and New England (and who knows how many disgruntled others?) would follow suit. If it still had the military means and the loyalty of the remaining troops, it might be expected to contrive a way (a Gulf of Tonkin or WMD excuse) to justify the invasion of a secessionist nation.

And yet, and yet. It is hard to think that a Federal government would actually command its troops to mow down Los Angelenos and San Franciscans the way they do the innocents of Fallujah and Najaf, or withstand the barrage of criticism, domestic and international, if it did; such an act would more likely propel additional secessions than gain support. It is harder still to think that the troops would actually carry out such an order, killing (ex)Americans on (ex)American territory. And if the troops did actually succeed in conquering and occupying an independent state, the population would be virtually uncontrollable—if it is not possible to win the hearts and minds of Vietnamese and Iraqis by invasion, think how much less possible it would be to win over people who had voted for secession with the full knowledge that it might lead to war,

It is not fantastic, then, to imagine that instead of a futile war Washington would be willing to negotiate a settlement, in the hopes that, by giving concessions on autonomy and self-regulation, say, and by demonstrating the extent of the Federal dollars lost, it could win a secessionist state back into the Union. In some cases, that might well happen, and if it failed it would at least show a government intelligent and confident enough to act as a future ally rather than a marauding warmonger. And as an ally, it might be able to establish diplomatic and trade ties that would allow it to still use such resources and talents of the new state as it wanted, perhaps even the bases it had previously used. With the additional benefit of no longer having to maintain Federal offices, regulators, highways, parks, dams, and such, and even presumably with a negotiated fee in compensation for these lost assets.

There is another strategy that a Federal government determined to squash secession might take, involving no troops, no war, nothing but a few phone calls. Washington might put pressure on large chain operations—Wal-Mart, Target, McDonald's, General Motors, Gannett, and many others—to cease doing business in the secessionist state, lest the Feds make things difficult for them in all the others. And unless the secession is so widespread that more states are out than in, a highly unlikely outcome, the corporations will comply and shut down and withdraw their businesses in the independent state.

Would that—or even the threat of that—cut the legs out from under a secessionist state and force it to come crawling back to the Union? I think not, for several reasons.

First, a seceding state would have to be, and would want to be, in great measure self-sufficient, providing for itself those goods and services it could not trade for with the outside world. Like Japan historically, and a number of other new states, it would create a phenomenon that Jane Jacobs has called "import replacement," the building of bicycles at home, recycling the metals and materials from the dumps and by the wayside, instead of buying them from abroad. It would certainly not be able to offer bikes for sale as cheaply as Wal-Mart does, at least at first, but it would put many more people to work per bike than Wal-Mart, and strengthen its economy in ways that would eventually enable its people to buy the more expensive product. Imagine this going on for a host of other goods across the state, replacing those that can be made by intelligent recycling and manufacturing, refitting and reusing others, developing hand crafts as a substitute for machinery to create others, refusing to make those that are pointless, wasteful, environmentally harmful, or costly, and foregoing many that turn out after a while to be neither necessary nor desirable. Wal-Mart would not only not be missed, it would be seen as having been a foolish enterprise that foisted too much needless "stuff," in too many useless varieties, of too shoddy a manufacture, with too much added-in transportation costs, on a gullible and malleable public.

And if the citizens of the new state really missed some big chain store and couldn't work out a replacement, they would stoically bear that burden as good and loyal patriots.

A second reason that the economic threat would not have much force is that the new state might well start out with more money in its coffers because it would not have to pay Federal income, gasoline, telephone, and other taxes; seventeen states (twelve of them "blue," interestingly enough) now pay more to the Federal government than they get back in Federal benefits. California, for example, got back just 78 cents in benefits for every dollar it sent to Washington in 2003 (according to the Tax Foundation), and as the independent Republic of California would thereby have an extra 22 cents in its pocket for every dollar—that would have meant, in 2004, that the citizens would have $88,000,000 lying around that wouldn't be going to Washington and they could use for local projects. Sounds like a pretty nice cushion to me.

Of course, not every state is California, and the attempt at some sort of economic independence would work out differently in different places—and if it looked like a state couldn't be on its own economically it would be very foolish to launch a secessionist movement. But a great many states in this country could be economically viable on their own, with arrangements that would let them trade with outside nations, including the U.S. and Canada. Besides, the necessity of economic survival is a very fertile mother, and like many small nations an independent state could find ways of making itself useful in the economic world; indeed, some of the richest nations—Liechtenstein, Luxembourg, Monaco, Cayman Islands, Iceland, Belgium, San Marino, and Singapore, for example— are some of the smallest, and that's leaving aside the Persian Gulf oil states.

The last reason for being optimistic about small-state viability, and the nullity of the Wal-Mart strategy, has to be put in the context of the economic future of the United States. I happen to be among the growing band of people who believe that there will be extremely difficult times ahead, and in the nearer rather than farther future, as a combination of crises and calamities pushes us to a completely new kind of society. They include the dwindling of cheap oil supplies (which already seems to have begun) and skyrocketing gasoline prices, the collapse of the value of the dollar from the spiraling trade deficit and national debt, the bursting of the real estate bubble, the effect of global warming on agriculture and fisheries, the rise of sea levels, the spread of diseases old and new, the increase in severe weather (of which Katrina is a foretaste), the diminution of fresh water, the exhaustion of tropical forests, the erosion of arable soils, the continued pollution of air and water, the depletion of mineral resources, and the whole impact of human activity on the global environment ("*Human activity is putting such a strain on the natural functions of Earth that the ability of the planet's ecosystems to sustain future generations can no longer be taken for granted*": Ecosystem Millennium Assessment, March 2005).

As a result of all that—or indeed of any of several parts of that—the national economy will have to transform itself. It will in fact be less a national than a local economy, particularly as gasoline supplies diminish and become prohibitively expensive and the dollar becomes an increasingly irrelevant measure of worth. James Howard Kunstler, whose new book The Long Emergency is about the likelihood of just such a future, writes that it will require us to downscale and re-scale virtually everything we do and how we do it, from the kind of communities we physically inhabit to the way we grow our food to the way we work and trade the products of our work….Anything organized on the large scale, whether it is government or a corporate business enterprise such as Wal-Mart, will wither as the cheap energy props that support bigness fall away. And then a small independent state, which can be more or less buffered from the national emergency and dependent on a relatively self-sufficient economy, makes a lot of sense.

Which might be the best argument for secession right there. If the future is going to be anything like what we alarmists are saying, there would seem to be a need to establish small-scale institutions and enterprises and trading circles as soon as possible, along with revivified community enterprises and cottage craftsmanship, and a statewide level suggests itself as the appropriate scale. And if that can be done in connection with political and cultural independence, such economic independence makes a powerful and attractive package. More than that, perhaps a necessary one.

Necessary, and, I want to argue, desirable. This country simply is not working right—as both the war in Iraq and the bumbling of Katrina (at all levels) make clear—and its corruption and inefficiency are harmful to the bulk of the population. The Federal government, aside from being bureaucracy-bound and politically hamstrung, is too big and complicated and inherently incompetent, and its attempt to provide for 280 million people and maintain a global empire of 725 military bases has proved to be impossible, placing terrible political and financial burdens on everyone. Secession would allow populations to escape this Leviathan, keep its human and financial resources from going down that rathole, avoid association with the failed politics of an ugly empire, and set its own policies (on same-sex marriage, abortion, stem-cell research, and so on) without interference from a distant central government increasingly in the hands of corporate interests and right-wing ideologues. It would allow a blue state a chance to escape from the policies and culture of a red-state government and set its own course. It would, in short, allow people to leave the country they dislike without leaving the homes they cherish. What could make more sense?

Secessionist No. 14: Seeing Red— and Seeing Blue

By Kirkpatrick Sale of the Middlebury Institute

It doesn't take more than a moment's reflection to realize that the United States is not. United, that is.

Not on any serious political, social, economic, or cultural issue that has come before us over the past several decades. Not even on what issues are important, or on how to solve them, or on who should tackle them.

Let's look at them. Immigration, border protection, guest workers. English as the official language. Iraq war/ withdrawal. War contracts and profiteering. Defense posture. Imperialism, foreign bases worldwide. War on terror. Torture and detention. Renditions. *Habeus corpus*. Government collection of phone and email data. Wiretapping without a warrant. Patriot Act. Independent judiciary. Government by secrecy. Federal legitimacy. Lawmaking by lobbyists. States' rights. Tax cuts for the rich. Port security.

Capital punishment. Death-row juveniles. Gun control. Stem-cell research. Right-to-die (Schiavo) plug-pulling. Assisted suicide. Evolution/creationism. Homosexual rights. Same-sex unions. Federal marriage amendment. AIDS research. Abortion. Condoms. Sexual abstinence as policy. Medical marijuana. Federal universal health care. Plan-B pills. Social Security. Medicare drug program. Balanced budget. Minimum wage.

Religion/evangelicals. Armageddon/Rapture. Faith-based Federal funding. Patriotism. Flag-burning. Environmental protection. Endangered species. Roadfree wilderness. Extractive industries. Global warming. Kyoto accords. Alternative energy. Wind towers. Nuclear power. Avian flu. Scientific research. Mileage fuel standards. Control of auto and power-plant emissions. Peak oil. Oil diplomacy.

United Nations. Test-ban treaties. Geneva Convention. International criminal court. NAFTA/globalization. Free trade. Europe. Dafur. Israeli occupation, settlements, and the wall. Palestinian intifada. Iranian nuclear program. Afghan warlords, poppy trade. Chinese oppression. Trade deficits.

And the right of states of the union to secede peaceably.

I've probably left out one or two, but you get the idea. On all of the serious issues of our time, and some not so monumental, the divisions of opinion (and sometimes multiple divisions) are wide and deep and contentious. They do not break down by party affiliation especially, or age, or gender, or wealth. There is some correlation between urban/rural, but not on all the issues. They break down mostly, as the last two elections have shown, by geography: the red states vs. the blue, the South, the Prairie, and the Rockies vs. New England, Middle Atlantic, the Great Lakes, and the West Coast.

It's not a perfect fit, of course, because presidential voters didn't vote on all these issues, only on the candidates, and those mostly avoided taking stands or took roughly similar positions. But let me look at the red-blue divisions on a number of key issues to show part of the general pattern.

The first and most remarkable issue is slavery. Yes, and I mean pre-Civil War slavery. All of the states that permitted slavery, and the four western territories where it was not outlawed (Kansas, Nebraska, Utah, New Mexico), voted red in the 2004 election. The states and territories where slavery was illegal (and blacks generally made unwelcome, or confined to towns like Indians to reservations), voted blue, with the exception of Ohio and Indiana, and the eastern part of the Washington and Oregon territories (which became Idaho). Can there be some lingering connection?

It is certainly not that black populations voted red, for the large majority went Democratic, so is it possible that places that developed a resentment of the North and the free states in and after the Civil War still have a deep tradition, and culture, of hostility to the rest of the nation, the effete East and the Left Coast, and what they would think of as the quiche and chardonnay crowd? And they express it by voting against the party strongest in these Democratic strongholds, and the candidates from them, instead voting for Republicans who are strong in the South and the Prairie states. In fact, you could argue that they have chosen to have native sons of this area become president, regardless of party, since 1977 (Carter, Reagan, Bush, Clinton, Bush, mindful that Reagan was a transplanted Californian).

But perhaps we should touch on more recent contentious issues. Take abortion: the states that have laws protecting this right are California, Connecticut, Maine, Maryland, Minnesota, Montana, Nevada, New Jersey, and Washington, and the states where courts have recognized the right are Illinois and Oregon. Almost all the states with the highest rates of abortion are blue, led by New York, Delaware, and Washington, and the red states have the lowest, with Utah, Idaho, and Colorado ranked last.

Or gay marriage/unions. The only states that allow it are California, Connecticut, Hawaii, Maine, Massachusetts, New Jersey, and Vermont with bills or court cases pending in New York and Rhode Island; all the other states but New Mexico have prohibitions against it, including the blue states of the Great Lakes.

Stem-cell research. The only states with laws or money supporting this are California, Connecticut, Illinois, Maryland, Massachusetts, and New Jersey, with Missouri considering a proposal for it. Power-plant emissions. States that have sued the Federal Environmental Protection Agency to raise standards on CO2 pollutants are Connecticut, Maine, Massachusetts, New Mexico, New York, Oregon, Rhode Island, Vermont, and Wisconsin.

Fuel efficiency. Not coincidentally, the same states plus California and New Jersey have also sued the EPA for tougher mileage regulations on SUVs and trucks. States that are planning to follow California's tough new fuel standards for these vehicles are Connecticut, Maine, Massachusetts, New Jersey, New York, Oregon, Pennsylvania, Rhode Island, Vermont, and Washington.

And on it goes. The blue states really are different. The same kinds of divisions hold true for countless other issues, ratified by poll after poll that have geographic breakdowns. The blue states, for one thing, are richer than the red—the top five states in per capita income are Connecticut, New Jersey, Massachusetts, Maryland, and New York, the bottom five are Utah, New Mexico, West Virginia, Arkansas, and Mississippi. Blue states pay far more to the Federal government than they get in return; all the red states except Colorado, Georgia, Nevada, and Texas get more money than they put in, and in some cases (New Mexico, Alaska, West Virginia, Mississippi, North Dakota, Alabama, Virginia, and Missouri) more than $1.50 back for every dollar in taxes.

Blue state people marry later and have a lower divorce rate, where people in the South have a divorce rate of 50 percent over the national average. Blue states have far more households with unmarried people, the most being in Maine, New Hampshire, and Vermont, the least in Alabama, Arkansas, and Mississippi. Best of all, blue states produce 95 percent of the quality wine and drink more of it than anyone else.

But what sense does all of this make—why should such a divided country stay together? To whose advantage, except the Federal politicians and the bureaucrats, and maybe the corporations that benefit from the commerce clause and uniform regulations? Is that enough?   Why on earth do people want to live under the same government with other people so dramatically different? Why do they want to keep fighting these battles? And why, when one side's preferences win out—as at present with the red states in power in Washington—should people suffer to live under laws and regulations and directives and practices that enshrine values and beliefs that they detest? Where is the moral, or philosophical, much less political, justification for such a system?

Isn't it obvious that a dissolution of this system would be to the advantage of all? The evangelicals wouldn't have to live with the godless, the pro-choice people wouldn't have to keep fighting the pro-lifes, the families frightened by homosexuality wouldn't have to worry about Will and Grace, the creationists could have their intelligent and other designs all to themselves without threat of Darwinists, the people who find the Iraq war not only illegal but inane wouldn't have to send their sons and daughters, the states that want to follow Kyoto protocols and establish wind farms and strictly oversee organic standards wouldn't have to follow a government that doesn't.

I'm not saying that with dissolution there would no longer be disagreements, for in no state is there probably unanimous agreement on any issue. But it would allow for the settling of a great many disputatious questions, and obviously add to the sum total of happiness thereby. Besides, once a state, or group of states (I'd think of New England for the blues, the Confederacy for the reds), did not have to worry about the other side and could go about running things as they saw fit, those who disagreed with these policies could up and leave, and those in other states who liked them could move in.

It's all so logical. The wonder is that it isn't happening right now across the land.

Second Edition Commentary
By Barry Lee Clark

Unlike most of the contributors to this work, Mr. Kirkpatrick Sale is a liberal. He is also a long-time advocate for more local rule, devolution and secession. His points in the previous article reiterate my comments on Michael Pierce's contribution. The United States is not at all united and is becoming less so. *Seeing Red, Seeing Blue*, was predictive its commentary on the growing divide. The issues Sale mentions still divide us. Certainly, the pendulum of gay marriage he discussed has swung in a different direction, but the only real change is one minority opinion was supplanted by a different minority opinion. In a nation so large as the United States there are always winners and losers on such fundamental issues.

But why must it be so?

Certainly, it would seem that if there were no "incorporation doctrine" created by the misreading of the unlawfully enacted 14th Amendment then the first nine amendments would serve only to restrict the Federal government. We would be free, in our states to elect governments that enacted laws closer to our values. California could be California and Alabama could be Alabama.

As Dr. Forrest MacDonald points out in his piece, nobody really wants to talk about the 14th Amendment. That leaves us with two choices in the United States. We can accept that we will live in a system that invariably will represent the views of a growing group of diverse minority opinions or we can seriously talk about ways and means to reorganize ourselves.

Secessionist No. 15: 'Things Fall Apart,' Ready or Not

By Kirkpatrick Sale of the Middlebury Institute
(Adbusters, January 2006)

We might as well admit it: as Yeats put it, "things fall apart, the center cannot hold,." If you want to know the dominant political trend of the moment, and the most likely political and economic scenario of the future, there it is.

On the global sphere, things have been falling apart in a sweeping way since 1945. The five empires that existed then—English, French, Spanish, Portuguese, and Soviet—have all collapsed, spinning off scores of smaller, independent states. The United Nations began with 51 nations in 1945, today it has 193. Czechoslovakia has split in two, Yugoslavia in seven (counting Kosovo and Montenegro). And there are strong and serious movements for the further breakdown of nations in Catalonia, Basque country, Scotland, Lapland, Sardinia, Sicily, Sudan, Congo, Kashmir, Aceh, Chechnya, Dagestan, South Osetttia, Kurdistan, Quebec, British Columbia, and some Indian nations of North America.

It's not too much to say that imperialism and globalism have failed—that's the thrust of John Ralston Saul's recent The Collapse of Globalism—and the nation state has become resurgent, though in many places on a smaller scale.   The strength of many of the new smaller nations is in fact what has been called nationalism, arguing a basic unity of culture and society that supports the political identity, as in, for example, Croatia, Slovenia, Kazakstan, and Georgia.

That is the trend, and it is by and large a good one, toward greater freedom, greater autonomy, and in some cases greater democracy. It has proved that smaller states are economically viable for the most part, a lesson that Liechtenstein, Luxemburg, Monaco, Cayman Islands, Iceland, Belgium, Oman, San Marino, and Singapore, among others, gave proof of long ago. Indeed, in many cases it is the separation itself that has spurred economic life, since new institutions and administrators are required and new goods and services are created to replace those provided by outsiders.

This is even the trend, in a nascent way, even in the United States, where there are by my count at least 28 separatist organizations, some decades old, as in Alaska and Hawaii, some formed in response to the 2004 Presidential "election," as in California and Michigan. The Vermont secessionist movement, begun essentially as an anti-Iraq war group in 2003, has nearly a thousand members now, has pushed through a state law for the annual observation of the day Vermont became an independent nation in 1777, and has even conducted a convention to put the case for secession in the State House in the capital, Montpelier. And it has spun off a think-tank, the Middlebury Institute, beginning this fall for "the study of separatism, secession, and self-determination" in the U.S. and beyond.

Whether or not secession in the U.S. is practical, as a number of perfectly serious hard-headed people are saying, may not actually even be an important question—it may simply become necessary. For one thing, as hurricane Katrina has glaringly shown, the Federal government is a clumsy, bureaucratic, politicized, and insensitive instrument (and as the rebuilding will show, corrupt as well), and states and localities that give themselves over to depending on it are in real trouble. If communities or states want to survive an emergency of any kind, they are going to have to develop agencies and institutions of their own, grounded in local realities, resources, and capabilities. This is exactly what a secessionist state would be best able to develop, at an efficient and democratic scale.

For another, an increasing crowd of people is predicting that an economic crunch is coming, made up of dwindling oil supplies, sky-high gasoline prices, severe weather crises, global warming dislocations, collapse of the dollar, and unsupportable national debt, and will be upon us faster than we think. And if that happens, none of the global and national systems and corporations that now dominate the economy will be able to survive. The global economy will collapse, and take the American empire down with it, and the Great Depression of the 1930s will look like prosperity.

It is then that smaller political and social units will be essential for survival and will arise where people have the sense and strength to establish self-sufficient and self-directing polities, whether they be states (or confederations of states), bioregions, cities, or communities. It is then that state secession will make sense in a multitude of ways, not only desirable as a means of extraction from the crumbling national economy but necessary as a means of concentrating on the development of local resources for local needs. And it becomes possible because the national apparatus will be essentially powerless to prevent it.

Of course, it would be easiest to shrug off the impending doom as the predictions of madmen and malcontents, and go about business as usual, fueling the $700 trillion national debt and the $200 billion trade deficit and assuming oil production will never peak. But it would be terribly foolish. The only sensible thing to do is to start thinking now about ways to survive and even thrive at a smaller scale. James Howard Kunstler, who has analyzed the coming crunch in his new book, The Long Emergency, has said that the new economy will require us to downscale and re-scale virtually everything we do and how we do it, from the kind of communities we physically inhabit to the way we grow our food to the way we work and trade the products of our work. Our lives will become profoundly and intensely local.

It would only prudent to start figuring out now just how to make that economy work, what resources we have in our immediate area and how they can best be utilized, what kinds of governance we would need and at what levels.

Things fall apart, and now secession begins to make a lot of sense.

Secessionist No. 17: What Is Secession?

By Donald W. Livingston
Originally Posted on VTCommons in Issue 7 - November 2005

Talk about secession makes Americans nervous. For many it evokes images of the Civil War, and is emotionally (if not logically) tied to slavery, war, and anarchy. That the word "secession" is laden with these negative connotations should be surprising since America was born in an act of secession. The Declaration of Independence is a secession document justifying an act whereby "one people...dissolve the Political Bands which have connected them with another." George Washington, John Adams, and Thomas Jefferson were secessionists. Americans should be the last people in the world embarrassed by the thought of secession. To understand both why secession is at the heart of the American political tradition and why Americans are nervous about it, we need to review the strange history of the idea.

The first thing to appreciate is that the meaning of the term "secession," as it is understood today, is no older than the late 19th century, and was forged in America. If I should stop someone on the street and ask whether he thinks secession is ever justified, the person might not have a ready answer, but he would know what I was asking. He would have an image of a people withdrawing from one political jurisdiction in order to form one of their own. For us the term "secession" has uniquely political connotations. But it was not always so.

The term derives from the Latin *secedere*, meaning merely an act of withdrawal, which is what "secession" meant until the 19th century. One could speak of the soul seceding from the body, or of seceding to the drawing room, or of seceding from the town to the country. To ask someone in 1760 whether he thinks secession is ever justified would be to draw a blank look. It would be like asking whether withdrawal is ever justified. When did "secession" cease to be a neutral term of withdrawal and become the name of a substantial political act?

Intimations of a change occurred in 1733 when the Scottish Church split. Those who left called themselves "seceders," and their church the "Secession Church." This church lasted nearly a century before splitting, but was soon reunited in 1829 under the paradoxical name of the "United Secession Church." Here the term "secession" means not simply withdrawal but a religious-political act whereby a people dismember a religious jurisdiction to form one of their own. It also means the celebration and remembrance of that act by naming the new way of life the "Secession Church." For the first time the term acquires substantial moral connotations. To be a seceder is a good thing. Though not strictly political, this religious-political connotation was familiar to an American Protestant culture for over a century, before it began to take on political connotations. The Oxford English Dictionary locates the first political use of the term in a statement by Thomas Jefferson in 1825 that colonies had seceded from the British Union.

But there were earlier uses. Indeed, throughout the entire antebellum period, and in every section of the federation, prominent American leaders considered withdrawal of their state or states from the federation as a policy option. The section that most often considered withdrawing was New England: in 1803 over the Louisiana Purchase, in 1808 over the embargo of British trade, in 1814 over the war with Britain, in 1843 over the annexation of Texas, and in 1847 over the Mexican War. No sooner was the Constitution ratified by the states than debate began about the viability of the federation and the legal and moral conditions a state would have to satisfy to withdraw from the federation. For seventy years this discourse was hammered out and given considerable theoretical refinement. The result was the transformation of the term "secession" to refer to a substantial political act about which one could be for or against.

This discourse about secession was uniquely American. From the mid-17th century on, European political speech had been mainly the language of centralization and unification; of building larger and larger centralized states, and even empires. This disposition to centralize did not diminish with the overthrow of monarchy, but increased dramatically with the emergence of mass democracy. The French Revolution sought to establish individual liberty through a massive centralization of power which ruled out competing jurisdictions. The American Revolution, by contrast, sought to promote individual liberty through a polycentric order of competing jurisdictions where secession was a policy option of last resort. Prior to the Civil War, "secession" in America described a political act, conceived of in a morally neutral way: secession might be a good or bad thing depending on the circumstances. After the war, it would acquire exclusively negative connotations. How are we to understand this change?

Although it is morally flattering to think the war was fought to emancipate slaves, the reason actually given by Lincoln and political and military leaders was that secession had to be defeated in order to preserve the central government's authority, which increasingly became identified with a new thing called the "nation." Previously the central government had been viewed as a service agency of the federation, whose main tasks were to treat with foreign countries, establish free trade among the states, and provide for their defense. The United States were regularly referred to in the plural. After the war the United States would be referred to in the singular.

Lincoln explained his reasons for invasion in a letter to Horace Greeley on August 22, 1862: "My paramount object in this struggle is to save the Union, and is not either to save or to destroy slavery." General Grant (a slaveholder who refused to free his slaves after the war until forced to do so by the 13th Amendment) had said that if the war was about emancipation, he would take his sword to the other side. But why was it so important to establish a territorial monopoly on coercion in Washington? Was not the continent large enough for two federations, or even more? Lincoln's answer was given in his First Inaugural: "Plainly, the central idea of secession, is the essence of anarchy." Why? Because, he said, if a part of the Union is allowed to secede, that part itself can be divided, and a part of that part, and so on which would mean the unraveling of government as such.

In his speeches, Lincoln presented the war as a world-historic struggle between the forces of republican government and the forces of anarchy. Most northern leaders who supported the war concurred. But many Northerners opposed the war. The Founding Jeffersonian tradition was still alive, and at least a third of the North was against the war, and another third was indifferent. To give just one example: Horace Greeley, editor of the Republican New York Tribune, declared on February 23, 1861, after a Confederacy of seven states had been formed: "We have repeatedly said...that the great principle embodied by Jefferson in the Declaration of Independence, that governments derive their powers from the consent of the governed, is sound and just; and that if...the cotton States, or the gulf States only, choose to form an independent nation, they have a clear moral right to do so. Whenever it shall be clear that the great body of Southern people have become conclusively alienated from the Union, and anxious to escape from it, we will do our best to forward their views."

The war to suppress secession was largely the work of Lincoln and the Republican Party (the founding party of state capitalism), which is why unconstitutional measures were necessary, such as destroying and arresting the editors of some 300 opposition newspapers and suspending the writ of habeas corpus for the duration of the war in the North, which netted around 20,000 political prisoners. Lincoln even wrote an order for the arrest of the Chief Justice of the Supreme Court, who had ruled against suspending the writ of habeas corpus. Mussolini, in his most vigorous years, in a larger country, and with a more efficient police system, rounded up only 12,000 political prisoners.

Although Lincoln's argument that secession means anarchy is incompatible with the American Founding, it fitted nicely with European thinking and practice, which for over two centuries had been building centralized states with territorial monopolies on coercion. The American polycentric order which allowed competing jurisdictions among sovereignties was viewed as antiquated and even as medieval. Nothing short of a violent revolution would be needed. With the triumph of the "Indivisible Union," it appeared to many Europeans that America had finally become a modern state. The editor of London's Spectator wrote triumphantly on December 22, 1866, that "The American Revolution marches fast towards its goal—the change of a Federal Commonwealth into a Democratic Republic, one and indivisible."

The Civil War was the bloodiest war of the 19th century. Europeans were shocked, and the lesson many drew from it was that secession necessarily leads to war and must be prevented at all cost. This threat was especially real in 19th-century Europe, where monarchies were being challenged in favor of republicanism and nationalism, and where everyone was talking about self-government and liberty. James Bryce, in his magisterial The American Commonwealth (1888), argued that secession caused the Civil War. Secession was possible because Americans had a defective constitution that did not centralize political authority. The argument of Lincoln, Bryce, and European elites (though there were notable European exceptions, including Goethe, Proudhon, and Lord Acton) that political power must be centralized, and competing jurisdictions eliminated, was uppermost in the minds of the founders of the Australian Constitution (1900) and the Canadian constitution, called The British North America Act (1867). Both constitutions go out of their way to make clear that the federal units of the respective regimes are artificial creatures of the central authority and devoid of sovereignty. In this way, they hoped to prevent an American-type war to suppress secession in Australia or Canada. To sum up. By the mid-nineteenth century, Americans, in debates over the meaning of the states' moral and legal relation to the Union, had transformed the meaning of the term "secession" from any act of withdrawal to a substantial political act. In the meantime, the modern European state, which was being imported around the world, was becoming more insistent on the need to suppress competing jurisdictions and make explicit its territorial monopoly on coercion. The American Civil War (caused, it was thought, by secession) was a wakeup call to this increasingly global European state system. And so it was that the political meaning given to "secession" by Americans in the antebellum period became the global meaning. And given the ubiquity of the unitary state system, this meaning was necessarily a negative one. Until the late 20th century, centralization and unification— however violently pursued—were generally

thought to be good things; secession and division—
however peacefully pursued—bad things.

But after a century of global wars of unprecedented
destruction and intensity, along with totalitarian
revolutions in which modern states killed more of their
own people than were killed in both world wars, the
mystique of centralization no longer has the authority it
had in the early 19th century. After the peaceful
secession of fifteen Soviet republics and other successful
secessions, the term "secession" is beginning to acquire
the morally neutral meanings it had in American prior to
the Civil War. But this means that the modern unitary
state, which has dominated political thought and
existence for three and a half centuries, is beginning to
lose its legitimacy.

The classical theory of the modern state is to be found
in Thomas Hobbes' Leviathan (1651). Hobbes argued
that the innate tendency of mankind is centrifugal and
violent. Without an artificial corporation having a
monopoly on coercion in a territory, there can be no
long-term peace and stability. Secession, in this theory,
is logically ruled out, and it is easy to see why. The
secession of a group within the state could be justified
only as the aggregate right of the individuals making up
the group. But if that aggregate could secede, so could
any other, down to one individual, and that would
contradict the very idea of the state.

Most modern theorists follow Hobbes in thinking of political society as artificial and held together by coercion. The classical statement of the counter tradition is that of Aristotle, who taught that political society is natural and occurs spontaneously, as does the family, society, and natural languages. Neither of these requires an all-powerful artificial corporation to maintain its existence. The enforcement mechanisms are internal to the practices themselves. Just what the bonds are that hold a political society together must be a topic for another day, but that such bonds exist should be obvious from the following examples, which refute Lincoln's claim—itself a Hobbesian theorem—that "secession is the essence of anarchy."

When the American colonies seceded from Britain they did not disintegrate into the endless secessions Lincoln feared. Kentucky would later secede from Virginia, Tennessee from North Carolina, Maine from Massachusetts, without further fragmentation. Norway seceded from Sweden (1905); Belgium from Holland (1830); Singapore from the Malaysian Federation (1965); and the vast Soviet Union peacefully dissolved in 1990. In none of these cases did Lincolnian or Hobbesian anarchy occur in the seceding units.

The Hobbesian picture is also static. Once a regime is established it remains indivisible.

But on the Aristotelian view, political societies naturally emerge in the world. Consequently, over time, a new political society might emerge within a larger one, demanding recognition, and even the right to secede. What are the criteria for recognizing when these conditions have been satisfied? I am afraid there is little philosophers can say about this; any more than they can provide criteria to know when two people should marry or when two people should divorce. All such judgments require what Aristotle called practical wisdom and a connoisseur's understanding of the people involved and the circumstances. But at least we can rule out the Hobbesian doctrine that secession should never occur, in favor of the Aristotelian doctrine that it is a contingent good to be determined by an act of practical wisdom. And perhaps we can go further and say that if a new political society has emerged that wishes to govern itself and is capable of doing so, and if secession imposes no serious injustice on the remaining polity, then the presumption must be on behalf of secession.

The case for secession is even more compelling in a federal system such as the United States, Canada, or the European Union, where the federative units are already recognized as political societies, with a functioning legislature, executive, judiciary, and other institutions needed to be an independent state.

The Hobbesian modern state is ubiquitous, and in its three-century-long career has transformed the meanings of political words, hiding from view or delegitimating other political possibilities. Nowhere is this clearer than in its perverse understanding of secession. The Hobbesian state demands a territorial monopoly on coercion in order to eliminate revolution and civil war within the border of the state. It defines secession as revolution or civil war, but this is fundamentally wrong. Revolution in modern political discourse has two meanings. One derives from John Locke; the other from the French Revolution, which I shall call Jacobin revolution. The purpose of Lockean revolution is to overthrow a government that has violated its fiduciary trust and perhaps to alter the structure of government. Jacobin revolution is much more than that. It is an attempt to reconstruct the entire social and political order. Both forms of revolution are acts that occur within a modern unitary state. And the same is true of civil war. The paradigm of civil war is the English Civil War in the 17th century, which was a battle between two factions seeking control of the central government. But secession is neither revolution nor civil war.

Secession is not Lockean revolution. It does not seek to overthrow or alter the government of a modern state, but seeks merely to limit its jurisdiction over the seceding territory. Nor is secession Jacobin revolution. It is not an attempt to entirely transform the social and political order of a modern state. Seceders typically have no interest in changing the social and political order of the region from which they wish to withdraw.

Nor is secession civil war. The seceding part of a polity is not engaged in a battle with the remaining part to control the central government of a modern state; it seeks merely to free itself from the jurisdiction of that government.

From these considerations, it follows that there was no American Revolution, but a war of secession. And there was no American Civil War, but a war to suppress secession. Failure to make these distinctions means that "secession" is governed by the logic of the Hobbesian modern state and always appears as either revolution or civil war and, consequently, as a form of violence to be legitimately suppressed. By calling secession revolution and the battle against it a civil war, the public (already conditioned to think in Hobbesian categories) will fail to see that the arguments that could justify suppressing revolution, in either Lockean or Jacobin form, do not and cannot apply to the quite different act of secession. Lincoln's justification for invading the Southern States was based on just this confusion of secession with revolution, which has ever since been an essential part of American historiography and even of American identity. Merely to recognize 1776 and 1861 as acts of secession rather than revolution or civil war would effect a revolution in the writing of American history and in American political self-understanding. Both of these landmark events are hostages of Hobbesian categories. But the Hobbesian state no longer has the legitimacy it once had. The claim that the state is indivisible is not a truth about the nature of political order as such, but an artifact of the 17th century, like farthingales, stockings, and the indestructible atom. The American Union never was and is not now indivisible. I mentioned the great constitutional efforts in the 19th century to prohibit secession by the Australian and Canadian Founders. Yet in 1931 Western Australia voted to secede. Quebec came close to voting for secession in 1995, and the Supreme Court of Canada recently ruled that a Canadian province has a right to secede.

Canada and the United States illustrate the impotence of the Hobbesian doctrine of indivisibility as well as the hubris of constitution-making. Canada began as a Hobbesian state which ruled out secession, but has evolved into a polity where the secession of a province is an acknowledged policy option. The United States began as a federation of sovereign states with the central government being little more than a service agency for the states, and where secession was entertained in every section as a policy option. Astonishingly, it has since evolved into a Hobbesian state said to be one and indivisible. Secession is a dialectical concept that cannot be understood without its opposite—the modern unitary state. The modern state cannot tolerate competing jurisdictions and demands a territorial monopoly on coercion; consequently, it absolutely rules out secession. As long as allegiance to the modern state was strong and people were confident of its worth (not only as an instrument but as an ideal), secession was a thoroughly negative concept. As the Hobbesian state and its ideology flourishes, so secession recedes in legitimacy. But as the state recedes in legitimacy, so secession flourishes. Since the end of the Cold War, we have entered a new period in which secession has again acquired the morally neutral connotations it had in its primordial appearance in antebellum America.

That public corporation known as the United States has simply grown too large for the purposes of self-government, in the same way that a committee of 300 people would be too large for the purposes of a committee. There needs to be a public debate on the outof-scale character of the regime and what can be done about it. This is the historic and noble task of the Second Vermont Republic. The long suppressed American idea of secession, as a public policy option, is returning to the United States as it came to the Soviet Union, Canada, Yugoslavia, Czechoslovakia, and other monsters created by a more than three-century-old policy of crushing hundreds of smaller polities into larger and larger monopolies of coercion.

Secessionist No. 18: Happy Secession Day

by Thomas J. DiLorenzo July 4, 2006
 originally posted on Lew Rockwell.com

Perhaps the best evidence of how American history was rewritten, Soviet style, in the post-1865 era is the fact that most Americans seem to be unaware that "Independence Day" was originally intended to be a celebration of the colonists' secession from the British empire. Indeed, the word secession is not even a part of the vocabulary of most Americans, who more often than not confuse it with "succession." The Revolutionary War was America's first war of secession.

America's most prominent secessionist, Thomas Jefferson, the author of the Declaration, was very clear about what he was saying: Governments derive their just powers from the consent of the governed, and whenever that consent is withdrawn, it is the right of the people to "alter or abolish" that government and "to institute a new government." The word "secession" was not a part of the American language at that time, so Jefferson used the word "separation" instead to describe the intentions of the American colonial secessionists.

The Declaration is also a states' rights document (not surprisingly, since Jefferson was the intellectual inspiration for the American states' rights political tradition). This, too, is foreign to most Americans. But read the final paragraph of the Declaration which states:

*That these United Colonies are, and of right ought to be,
FREE AND INDEPENDENT STATES; that they are
absolved from all allegiance to the British crown and that
all political connection between them and the state of
Great Britain is, and ought to be, totally dissolved; and
that, as free and independent states, they have full
power to levy war, conclude peace, contract alliances,
establish commerce, and do all other things which
independent states may of right do* (emphasis in
original).

Each colony was considered to be a free and
independent state, or nation, in and of itself. There was
no such thing as "the United States of America" in the
minds of the founders. The independent colonies were
simply united for a particular cause: seceding from the
British empire. Each individual state was assumed to
possess all the rights that any state possesses, even to
wage war and conclude peace. Indeed, when King
George III finally signed a peace treaty he signed it with
all the individual American states, named one by one,
and not something called "The United States of
America." The "United States" as a consolidated,
monopolistic government is a fiction invented by Lincoln
and instituted as a matter of policy at gunpoint and at
the expense of some 600,000 American lives during
1861–1865.

Jefferson defended the right of secession in his first
inaugural address by declaring, *"If there be any among
us who would wish to dissolve this Union or to change its
republican form, let them stand undisturbed as
monuments of the safety with which error of opinion
may be tolerated where reason is left to combat it."* (In
sharp contrast, in his first inaugural address, Lincoln
promised an "invasion" with massive "bloodshed" (his
words) of any state that failed to collect the newly-
doubled federal tariff rate by seceding from the union).

Jefferson made numerous statements in defense of the defining principal of the American Revolution: the right of secession. In a January 29, 1804 letter to Dr. Joseph Priestly he wrote:

Whether we remain in one confederacy, or form into Atlantic and Mississippi confederacies, I believe not very important to the happiness of either part. Those of the western confederacy will be as much our children & descendants as those of the eastern, and I feel myself as much identified with that country, in future time, as with this; and did I now foresee a separation [i.e., secession] at some future day, yet I should feel the duty & the desire to promote the western interests as zealously as the eastern, doing all the good for both portions of our future family which should fall within my power.

In an August 12, 1803 letter to John C. Breckinridge Jefferson addressed the same issue, in light of the New England Federalists' secession movement in response to his Louisiana Purchase. If there were a "separation" into two confederacies, he wrote, "God bless them both, & keep them in the union if it be for their good, but separate them, if it be better."

So on July 4 stoke up the grill, enjoy your barbecue, and drink a toast to Mr. Jefferson and his fellow secessionists. (And beware of any Straussian nonsense about how it was really Lincoln, the greatest enemy of states' rights, including the right of secession, who taught us to "revere" the Declaration of Independence. Nothing could be further from the truth.)

Thomas J. DiLorenzo is the author of *The Real Lincoln: A New Look at Abraham Lincoln, His Agenda, and an Unnecessary War*, (Three Rivers Press/Random House). *How Capitalism Saved America: The Untold Story of Our Country's History, from the Pilgrims to the Present* (Crown Forum/Random House, August 2004).

Secessionist Paper No. 19: The Right of Secession

by Gene H. Kizer, Jr.

There is no evidence that secession was illegal or prohibited by the Constitution, and in fact there is almost overwhelming evidence to the contrary, that secession was a legal, constitutionally sanctioned act. Historian Kenneth M. Stampp, in his book *The Imperiled Union*, maintains that it is impossible to say that secession was illegal because of the ambiguity of the original Constitution as to state sovereignty and the right of secession. He points out that "the case for state sovereignty and the constitutional right of secession had flourished for forty years before a comparable case for a perpetual Union had been devised," and even then its logic was "far from perfect because the Constitution and the debates over ratification were fraught with ambiguity." [62]   It appears that the original intent of an unquestioned right of secession was established by the Founders, took root and "flourished for forty years," then later a "perpetual Union" counter-argument developed out of political necessity when Northern states began realizing their wealth and power was dependent on the Union and its exploitation of the South.

There had to be a specific constitutional prohibition on secession for it to be illegal. Conversely, there did not have to be a specific constitutional affirmation of the right of secession for it to be legal. Why? Because the 10th Amendment to the United States Constitution states:

The powers not delegated to the United States by the Constitution, nor prohibited by it to the States, are reserved to the States respectively, or to the people. There was no constitution prohibition on secession, nor was there a constitutional sanctioning of any kind of federal coercion to force a state to obey a federal law because to do so was to perpetrate an act of war on the offending state by the other states, for whom the federal government was their agent.

   The arguments for the right of secession are compelling. There is the constitutional right based on the Compact Theory, and the revolutionary right based on the idea that a free people have the right to change their government anytime they see fit. The Compact Theory views the Constitution as a legal agreement between the states - a compact - and if any one state violates the compact, then the entire agreement becomes null and void. Northern states unquestionably violated the Constitution on a number of grounds including unconstitutional Personal Liberty Laws on their books, as well as by deliberately harboring fugitives from justice by protecting the sons of John Brown who were wanted by Virginia for murder at Harpers Ferry. Northern states also made a mockery of the Constitution's Preamble, which states clearly that the Constitution was established to "insure domestic Tranquility" and "promote the general Welfare." Certain prominent Northern leaders with the acquiescence of states like Massachusetts were utterly at war with the South and doing everything they could to destroy the domestic tranquility of Southern states by encouraging slaves to murder white people, poison wells, destroy property and commit other acts of rapine. John Brown himself had been encouraged and financed in the North.

   The revolutionary right of secession is based on the Declaration of Independence and the philosophy of Thomas Jefferson and John Locke, that whenever any form of government becomes destructive of the ends for which it was established, it is the right of the people to alter or abolish it, and to institute new government, ...

These words come directly from the Declaration of Independence. This passage was also used, verbatim, in South Carolina's Declaration of the Immediate Causes Which Induce and Justify the Secession of South Carolina from the Federal Union. A similar sentiment was expressed by Abraham Lincoln in 1847 on the floor of the United States House of Representatives:

"Any people, anywhere, being inclined and having the power, have the right to rise up and shake off the existing government, and form a new one that suits them better. This is a most valuable, a most sacred right, a right which we hope and believe is to liberate the world." [63]

Horace Greely's New York Daily Tribune published a long, emotional editorial on December 17, 1860, the day South Carolina's Secession Convention began, strongly supporting the right of secession on the revolutionary basis. The Tribune used the exact same passage used in South Carolina's Declaration of Immediate Causes, which comes from the Declaration of Independence, reiterating that the "just powers" of government come from the "consent of the governed" and "'whenever any form of government becomes destructive of these ends, it is the right of the people to alter or abolish it, and institute a new government.", adding that:

"We do heartily accept this doctrine, believing it intrinsically sound, beneficent, and one that, universally accepted, is calculated to prevent the shedding of seas of human blood. And, if it justified the secession from the British Empire of Three Millions of colonists in 1776, we do not see why it would not justify the secession of Five Millions of Southrons from the Federal Union in 1861." [64]

The Tribune goes on to say it "could not stand up for coercion, for subjugation," because:

"We hold the right of self-government sacred," and if the Southern States want out, "we shall feel constrained by our devotion to Human Liberty to say, Let Them Go!", because self-government is one of the "Rights of Man." [65]

   The States' Rights Hartford Convention of New England, aggrieved by the financial losses of New Englanders in shipping during the War of 1812, met in 1815 and seriously discussed seceding from the Union. [66] The Convention selected representatives to go to Washington to present its grievances to the government. It even chose a military leader should its grievances be ignored, and made arrangements for a second convention, if necessary, to make specific plans to secede. Commissioners were sent to Washington but upon arriving found that the War of 1812 had ended, therefore it was not necessary to air their grievances. The Journal of the Hartford Convention bristles with references to state sovereignty, and uses States' Rights language such as the right of a state to decide for itself when a violation of the Constitution occurred. One quote from the Hartford Convention Journal, justifying secession, sums it up:

"Whenever it shall appear that these causes are radical and permanent, a separation by equitable arrangement, will be preferable to an alliance by constraint, among nominal friends, but real enemies, inflamed by mutual hatred and jealousy, and inviting by intestine division, contempt and aggression from abroad."

Some excellent constitutional arguments are summarized in an article entitled "*The Foundations and Meaning of Secession*," by Mr. H. Newcomb Morse, in the Stetson Law Review, a publication of the Stetson University College of Law. Morse writes that the War Between the States did not prove that secession was illegal because many incidents both preceding and following the War support the proposition that the Southern States did have the right to secede from the Union. Instances of nullification prior to the War Between the States, contingencies under which certain states acceded to the Union, and the fact that the Southern States were made to surrender the right to secession all affirm the existence of a right to secede.

He adds that the Constitution's "failure to forbid secession" and amendments dealing with secession that were proposed in Congress as Southern states were seceding strengthened his argument that "the Southern States had an absolute right to secede from the Union prior to the War Between the States."

Morse argues that because the Constitution did not forbid secession, then every state acceding to the Constitution had the implied right to secede from it. He says that if men of the caliber of Madison, Hamilton and the others meant to forbid secession they definitely would have said so, and the omission of a prohibition on secession in the Constitution is strong proof that the right of secession existed and was assumed. He quotes James Madison from The Madison Papers who wrote "a breach of any one article by any one party, leaves all other parties at liberty to consider the whole convention as dissolved." Vermont and Massachusetts, he points out, nullified with statutes, the Fugitive Slave Law of 1793, and those two breaches of the compact alone were enough for the South to consider the compact dissolved.

There were many other violations of the Constitution discussed throughout the secession debate including Northern Personal Liberty Laws that, in effect, nullified the Fugitive Slave Law of the Compromise of 1850 as well as Article IV, Section 3 of the Constitution, which dealt with fugitive slaves. At least ten Northern states had statutes that nullified the two aforementioned laws. Other breaches of the Constitution included, as stated earlier, the harboring of fugitives from justice in the North, specifically two of John Brown's sons who were with Brown at Harpers Ferry and were wanted in Virginia for murder, but were being harbored in Ohio and Iowa. Brown himself had been encouraged by Northerners and financed by Northern money. Certain Northern leaders, again, with the acquiescence of states like Massachusetts, tried desperately to destroy "domestic Tranquility" in the South by sending incendiary abolitionist material in the mail encouraging slaves to revolt and murder. Lincoln's own Republican Party published 100,000 copies of Hinton Helper's The Impending Crisis, which called for slave revolt, and Republicans in Congress endorsed the book and used it as a campaign tool.

To prove the right of a state to determine for itself when the Constitution has been violated, Morse quotes Jefferson's Kentucky Resolutions which point out that if the government had the right to determine when the Constitution was violated, then the government would be the arbiter of its own power and not the Constitution. The Kentucky Resolutions also reaffirm state sovereignty and independence. [67]

Morse demonstrates that congressional discussions and proposed legislation during the secession of Southern states indicated that Congress believed the right of secession to exist. One piece of legislation was introduced to deal with the disposition of federal property within a seceding state, as well as a seceding state's assumption of its share of the national debt. Another scrambled to forbid secession unless approved by two-thirds of the members of both Houses of Congress, the president, as well as all the states. Morse then points out that thirty-six years earlier, Chief Justice John Marshall, in Gibbons v. Ogden wrote that "limitations of a power furnish a strong argument in favor of the existence of that power..." [68] He concludes:

"What would have been the point of the foregoing proposed amendments to the Constitution of the United States prohibiting or limiting the right of secession if under the Constitution the unfettered right of secession did not already exist? Why would Congress have even considered proposed amendments to the Constitution forbidding or restricting the right of secession if any such right was already prohibited, limited or non-existent under the Constitution?"

Morse goes on to discuss the conditional ratification of the Constitution by three of the original thirteen states, which carefully reserved the right of secession. They were Virginia, New York, and Rhode Island. Virginia used the exact wording of her conditional ratification of the U.S. Constitution, in her Ordinance of Secession. Morse points out that since the other states, which had unconditionally ratified the Constitution, consented to Virginia's conditional ratification, then they "ostensibly assented to the principle that Virginia permissibly retained the right to secede." He adds that with the additional acceptance of "New York's and Rhode Island's right to secede, the existing states of the Union must have tacitly accepted the doctrine of secession." Further, Morse states that according to the Constitution, all the new states that joined the Union after the first thirteen also had the right of secession since new states entered on an equal footing with the exact same rights as the existing states. [69]

Southerners during the secession debate knew and understood this argument. Senator Judah P. Benjamin of Louisiana, a brilliant legal mind who was later Attorney General, Secretary of War and Secretary of State of the Confederacy, in his farewell speech to the United States Senate on February 5, 1861, said:

"The rights of Louisiana as a sovereign state are those of Virginia; no more, no less. Let those who deny her right to resume delegated powers, successfully refute the claim of Virginia to the same right, in spite of her expressed reservation made and notified to her sister states when she consented to enter the Union." [70]

Morse skips forward to Reconstruction, and points out that "the Northern occupational armies were removed from Arkansas, North Carolina, Florida, South Carolina, Mississippi, and Virginia only after those former Confederate States had incorporated in their constitutions a clause surrendering the right to secede." Morse then argues brilliantly that by insisting that the former Confederate States surrender their right to secede, the United States government had implicitly admitted that those states originally had the right. How could they surrender a right, unless they had it in the first place? [71]

To summarize, Morse points out that before the war, under Virginia's conditional ratification of the Constitution, when the people decided that government power had been "perverted to their injury or oppression," they had the right to secede. When Northern states passed Personal Liberty Bills and other statutes nullifying the fugitive slave laws of the Constitution (Article IV, Section 3), a "perversion" occurred which gave the Southern states the right to secede. Reinforcing that "perversion" even further was the Federal government's not forcing those Northern states to abide by the Constitution, therefore the Northern States conceivably "perverted" national law to the "injury or oppression" of the people of the Southern States. Thus, the resumption of the powers of government by the people of the Southern States was a natural consequence of the Northern States' conduct and the federal government's failure to prohibit that conduct. [72]

The only other issue, according to Morse, was whether the Southern states conducted their act of secession legally. Morse points out that the people are the sovereign, having supreme, absolute and perpetual power, therefore secession would have to be accomplished by the people of each state rather than even the legislatures. He says "convention delegates elected by the people of the state to decide one question constitute authority closer to the seat of the sovereign -- the people themselves," therefore a convention in each Southern state would be necessary as a "special agent of the people of the state." Did the Southern states conduct themselves legally and therefore perfect their acts of secession and independence? Morse says:

"*When the Southern States seceded from the Union in 1860 and 1861, not one state was remiss in discharging this legal obligation. Every seceding state properly utilized the convention process, rather than a legislative means, to secede. Therefore, not only did the Southern States possess the right to secede from the Union, they exercised that right in the correct manner.*" [73]

Morse's conclusion is that "conceivably, it was the Northern States that acted illegally in precipitating the War Between the States. The Southern States, in all likelihood, were exercising a perfectly legitimate right in seceding from the Union." [74]

Other evidence of the right of secession abounds. Albert Taylor Bledsoe wrote in 1866 what is thought to be the best book ever written on the right of secession: Is Davis a Traitor; or Was Secession a Constitutional Right Previous to the War of 1861? Dr. Richard M. Weaver, who was, during his lifetime, a professor and author of several noted books on the South, called Is Davis a Traitor? "the masterpiece of the Southern apologias." Weaver described it as a "brilliant specimen of the polemic" out of the entire "extensive body of Southern political writing." [75]

Dr. Clyde N. Wilson, long time professor of history at the University of South Carolina, goes even further. In the Introduction to a 1995 reprint of *Is Davis a Traitor?*, Dr. Wilson lists the top seven books defending the South and the right of secession and says "Bledsoe did it first and best," his argument for the right of secession being "absolutely irrefutable to any honest mind." [76] The other six works that best defend the South and right of secession according to Dr. Wilson are the two-volume work *A Constitutional View of the Late War Between the States* by Alexander H. Stephens, *The Rise and Fall of the Confederate Government* by Jefferson Davis, *A Defence of Virginia and Through Her of the South* by Robert L. Dabney, *The Creed of the Old South* by Basil L. Gildersleeve, *The Southern States of the American Union Considered in their Relations to the Constitution of the United States and the Resulting Union* by Jabez L. M. Curry, and *The Lost Cause* by Edward A. Pollard.

According to Dr. Wilson in the Introduction, pages i-viii, Bledsoe was born in Frankfort, Kentucky, in 1809. He graduated from West Point in 1830 and had been there part of the time with Robert E. Lee, Jefferson Davis, Leonidas Polk and Albert Sydney Johnston. He loved mathematics and theology, but practiced law for nine years in Springfield, Illinois, as part of a bar that included Abraham Lincoln and Stephen A. Douglas. Dr. Wilson writes that "it was said that Bledsoe won six out of eleven cases tried against Lincoln," and that he had given Lincoln lessons, at one point, on using a broadsword because Lincoln had been challenged to a duel. After his legal career, Bledsoe taught astronomy and mathematics at the University of Mississippi, acquiring a "legendary" genius for mathematics. In 1854, he began teaching mathematics at the University of Virginia. During the war, Bledsoe served briefly as the colonel of a regiment of infantry from Virginia, then later in the Confederate War Department, and finally he was sent to Europe by President Davis on what is thought to have been a secret diplomatic mission to influence public opinion in Britain. After the war, until his death in 1877, Bledsoe published The Southern Review, in which he continued to argue the justice and truth of the Southern cause.

Bledsoe began working on *Is Davis a Traitor?* while in England and published it just after the war "as a part of the campaign of Davis's defense." The Confederate President was in a Yankee prison, Fortress Monroe, where he spent a miserable two years waiting to be tried for treason. He was in irons with a light shining brightly in his cell twenty-four hours a day and with Union guards marching back and forth. The bright light was an additional measure of Yankee viciousness since it was known that Davis had never been able to sleep except in total darkness.

Davis wanted to be tried for treason because he was confident he could prove the right of secession. However, he never got his chance, and that denial of Jefferson Davis' trial on the charge of treason by the Northern government is additional evidence of the right of secession.

In talking about the effectiveness of *Is Davis a Traitor?*, Richard Weaver writes that Bledsoe witnessed some practical result of his labor when Robert Oulds and Charles O'Conor, attorneys for Jefferson Davis, made use of the book in preparing their defense; but the Federal government, apparently feeling the weakness of its legal position, allowed the case to be dismissed. [77]

Here was the North's big chance to prove the South wrong once and for all in a solemn, dignified court of law in the eyes of the entire world and for all of posterity, but they refused to take it. Why? They certainly had not suddenly had a change of heart toward the South. It was Reconstruction, the body of the assassinated Lincoln was barely cold in the ground while the hateful Charles Sumner, no doubt still smarting from his caning by Preston Brooks, along with Thaddeas Stephens and other South hating radical Republicans were ascending in Congress. Northern troops were in control of every Southern government while large numbers of former Confederates were disfranchised.

This was exactly the time the federal government would have wanted to convict the Southern president if it had a case. The federal government was willing to kill hundreds of thousands of Southerners on the battle field, so there can be no doubt it would have relished humiliating Jefferson Davis in a courtroom. It is a virtual certainty that if the North's case had been strong they would have taken it to trial and vindicated their war against the hated South once and for all. That the Federal government did not go to court against the Confederate president after keeping him in jail for two years charged with treason, is strong evidence that there was indeed a legal right of secession and the South had exercised it properly. There were no other treason trials against former Confederates because any one trial would likely prove the legal right of secession, and imminently practical Northerners were not about to lose in a court of law what they had won on the battlefield.

Bledsoe's "irrefutable" argument in *Is Davis a Traitor?*" begins with the Constitution as a compact, or legal agreement among the members to the compact. The reason Bledsoe starts here is because any member that has acceded to (agreed to) the terms of a compact, can secede from that compact if the terms are broken by one of the other members. Bledsoe produces the writings and statements of the strongest opponents of the Constitution as compact - Daniel Webster and others - who have admitted that if the Constitution is a compact, then states can secede from it; but who deny that the Constitution is a compact. [78] Webster was the great spokesman for the North with the credibility and reputation to go along with it. Bledsoe writes:

"Thus, the great controversy is narrowed down to the single question -- Is the Constitution a compact between the States? If so, then the right of secession is conceded, even by its most powerful and determined opponents; by the great jurist, as well as by 'the great expounder' (Webster) of the North." [79]

The evidence that the North had broken the specific terms and spirit of the compact if it was a "compact," was substantial. As stated earlier, Northern states had statutes on their books nullifying the Constitutional and Congressional law with regard to fugitive slaves. Many other specific breaches of the Constitution by the North existed in areas besides slavery. Many in the North for over two decades believed, as Seward had clearly stated, that they were operating according to a "higher law" than the Constitution. The more radical had long called the Constitution a "covenant with death and agreement with hell." So, the North's having broken the compact virtually guaranteed that secession was legal if, indeed, the Constitution was a compact that was "acceded to" by the original makers. Did the original states "accede" to a compact?

Bledsoe attacks the arguments of Webster and the others one at a time taking on the strongest, most salient parts of their arguments. For example, Webster had said "words are things, and things of mighty influence." At one point, in the Senate, Webster had railed against the Constitution as compact. Webster had said that saying "the States acceded to the Constitution" was "unconstitutional language." Of course the reason he felt that way, as Bledsoe had said, was because if states had acceded to the Constitution, then it was only logical that they could secede from it. Discrediting the single word, "accede," was very important to Webster, so Bledsoe researched in great detail the words of the founders and finds that in the Constitutional Convention of 1787, *"Mr. James Wilson ... preferred 'a partial union' of the States, 'with a door open for the accession of the rest.'"* However, "Mr. Gerry, a delegate from Massachusetts, was opposed to *'a partial confederacy, leaving other States to accede or not to accede, as had been intimated.'"* Father of the Constitution, James Madison, *"used the expression 'to accede' in the Convention of 1787, in order to denote the act of adopting 'the new form of government by the States.'"* Virginia Governor Randolph, also at the Convention of 1787, had said *"That the accession of eight States reduced our deliberations to the single question of Union or no Union."* Patrick Henry had said that if the Constitution *"be amended, every State will accede to it."* Mr. Grayson asks if Virginia will gain anything from her prominent position *"by acceding to that paper."* Benjamin Franklin, whom Bledsoe says was next in importance at the Constitutional Convention to Washington, later said *"Our new Constitution is now established with eleven States, and the accession of a twelfth is soon expected."* George Washington, as he watched states join the Constitution, said *"If these, with the States eastward and northward of us, should accede to the Federal government . . .".* Chief Justice John Marshall used the word "accede" in reference to joining the Constitution, and even Mr. Justice Story, a staunch opponent of the belief in Constitution as compact, in agreement with Webster, said *"The Constitution has been ratified by all the States; . . . Rhode Island did not accede to it, until more than a year after it had been in operation;"*.

Webster had attacked the word "accede" as something invented by proponents of the Constitution as compact. His intention was to discredit his opponents by discrediting the language they were using, but his plan backfired. Bledsoe points out that Webster's attack on the word "accede" by calling it a "new word," was ill founded and incorrect because "accede" had precisely been "the word of the fathers of the Constitution" with Washington "at their head." They had all used the word "accede" in reference to states joining the Constitution, and of course, the converse of the word "accede," is "secede."

Over and over Bledsoe demolishes each and every argument that maintains secession was not legal or a right. To those like Webster, who tried to say the Constitution was not a compact, Bledsoe offers the words of the Father of the Constitution, James Madison, in the Virginia Resolutions of 1798, *"That this assembly doth explicitly and peremptorily declare, that it views the powers of the Federal Government as resulting from the compact, to which the States are parties."* Bledsoe further mentions a letter from Madison to a Mr. Everett in 1830 in which Madison says that the Constitution is *"'a compact among the States in their highest sovereign capacity.'"* Bledsoe then uses Webster's own words against him, quoting Webster admitting that the Constitution was a compact in a debate three-years earlier, on "Foote's resolutions." Bledsoe says:

"Mr. Webster himself, had, like everyone else, spoken of the Constitution as a compact, as a bargain which was obligatory on the parties to it. 'it is the original bargain,' says he, in that debate; 'the compact -- let it stand; let the advantage of it be fully enjoyed. The Union itself is too full of benefits to be hazarded in propositions for changing its original basis. I go for the Constitution as it is, and for the Union as it is.'"

Perhaps the strongest argument against the right of secession, is based on the wording in the Constitution's Preamble: "We the people." Those who argue that the Constitution is not a compact, but is a national document, believe that "We the People" means all of the American people in one body, and not in their sovereign states. This, says Bledsoe on page 61, *"is the great stronghold, if it has one, of the Northern theory of the Constitution. The argument from these words appears in every speech, book, pamphlet, and discussion by every advocate of the North. It was wielded by Mr. Webster in his great debate with Mr. Calhoun, in 1833, . . .".* If the Constitution was written as a document for all of the American people in one body, then individual states had no right to withdraw from it. The committee on style of the Constitutional Convention of 1787 was headed by Gouverneur Morris of Pennsylvania. Notwithstanding the Northern nationalist rhetoric, this is what Gouverneur Morris said was the meaning of the Constitution and those words, "We the people," that he had authored:

"The Constitution was a compact not between individuals, but between political societies, the people, not of America, but of the United States, each enjoying sovereign power and of course equal rights."

The "United States" means just that: states that are united. Morris himself believed in the right of secession and supported New England's move to secede during the War of 1812, which culminated in the Hartford Convention. Bledsoe quotes The Madison Papers and refers to some 900 pages of the proceedings of the Constitutional Convention of 1787, in which are recorded the debate over method of ratification. He points out that nowhere in that vast record is there a discussion of the "people" as meaning the entire American people outside of their states. The big debate was over whether the legislatures of each state would ratify the Constitution, or the "people" of each state in special convention. It was clearly "legislature vs people in convention" of each state. It was decided by the Constitutional Convention that since a later legislature might rescind the ratification of an earlier legislature, it would be a sounder foundation to have the people of each state ratify the Constitution in special conventions called for the purpose of ratification. This is exactly how the South seceded, by secession conventions called for the single purpose of deciding the issue of secession. And, as Mr. H. Newcomb Morse said in the Stetson Law Review, "not one state was remiss in discharging this legal obligation."

There was another problem in that nobody knew how many states, or which ones, would ratify the Constitution, therefore listing the specific states in the Preamble could not be done as it had been done in the body of the Articles of Confederation. If all the states had been listed and one refused to ratify, then the document would be invalid. The number "nine" was decided on, as the number of states necessary to put the Constitution into effect, but in debating the issue it was brought up that the Constitution could only apply to those states ratifying it, therefore no references could be made to "all" of the American people. Bledsoe writes that Rufus King suggested adding "between the said states, so as to confine the operation of the government to the States ratifying the same." The words were cleaned up and found their way into the Constitution in Article VII which starts out:

The Ratification of the Conventions of nine States, shall be sufficient for the Establishment of this Constitution between the States so ratifying the Same.

Bledsoe further clarifies by writing that "when it was determined that the Constitution should be ratified by 'the Conventions of the States,' and not by the legislatures, this was exactly equivalent, in the uniform language of the Convention of 1787, to saying that it shall be ratified by 'the people of the States.' Hence, the most ardent friend of State rights, or State sovereignty, saw no reason why he should object to the words, 'We, the people of the United States,' because he knew they were only intended to express the mode of ratification by the States . . . in their sovereign capacity, as so many political societies or peoples, as distinguished from their legislatures."

Bledsoe goes on by pointing out that the Federal government had no legal right whatsoever to coerce a state into following its laws therefore it had no right to force a seceding state back into the Union. President Buchanan had stated in his lame duck period between Lincoln's election of November 6, 1860, and March 4, 1861, when Lincoln would be inaugurated, while state after state was seceding, that as president of the United States, he had no power to coerce a state, even though he denied that secession was legal. Bledsoe notes the contradiction in Buchanan's position and writes "if we say, that coercion is a constitutional wrong, or usurpation, is not this saying that the Constitution permits secession, or, in other words, that it is a Constitutional right?" He says "Coercion is unconstitutional . . . wrong . . .strikes down and demolishes the great fundamental principle of the Declaration of Independence, -- the sacred right of self-government itself." About secession, he says "Secession, on the other hand, asserts the right of self-government for every free, sovereign, and independent State in existence."

Bledsoe discussed the views of credible foreigner observers and writes that Alexis de Tocqueville, in Democracy in America, said:

"The Union was formed by the voluntary agreement of the States; and in uniting together they have not forfeited their nationality, nor have they been reduced to the condition of one and the same people. If one of the States choose to withdraw from the compact, it would be difficult to disprove its right of doing so, and the Federal Government would have no means of maintaining its claims directly either by force or right." To Tocqueville, Bledsoe adds "Mackay, and Spence, and Brougham, and Cantu, and Heeren," then he goes on "as well as other philosophers, jurists and historians among the most enlightened portions of Europe, (who) so readily adopt the Southern view of the Constitution, and pronounce the American Union as a confederation of States." [80]

Bledsoe continues with more persuasive argument, the words of Thomas Jefferson and Alexander Hamilton, who assert, beyond doubt, that the Constitution is a compact and the states, sovereign. He discusses William Rawl of Philadelphia and his book, A View of the Constitution of the United States, which stresses the right of secession and was used at West Point during most of the antebellum era , and the State's Rights Hartford Convention of New England states, which strongly supported the right of secession. These are but a few of the arguments found in Bledsoe's persuasive book.

The Southern states did not rush headlong into secession. They had enormous grievances against the North that were much greater than even Northern violations of the Constitution. The unfairness of taxation, which had been the huge issue of the Revolution, was worse for the antebellum South because three-fourths of the taxes were paid by the South, while three-fourths of the tax money was spent in the North. It had held down the development of Southern industry for a half-century and Southerners were tired of it. Southerners felt the North was already at war with them in many ways. They saw Northern emissaries sent South to encourage slave uprisings, murder and rapine, then being applauded in the North for their grisly successes, especially John Brown. Southerners saw Hinton Helper's book, The Impending Crisis, which was full of errors on its economics, call for bloody slave revolt yet be enthusiastically adopted by the Republicans in Congress as a campaign document. With the election of Republican Lincoln, Southerners believed those same Republicans would now put into effect the principles of Helper's book, and there was nothing they could do about it. For their own safety, Southern states began debating secession. They did so peacefully and with great intellectual vigor and in the end, the people of the South struck for independence and self-government, just as their fathers in the Revolution had.

The North, however, had become wealthy manufacturing, shipping, and financing for the captive Southern market, which was rich itself because of King Cotton. The North could not let the South go without a complete economic collapse that was well underway during the secession winter and spring of 1860-1861. All the noble rhetoric of the Horace Greelys in 1860 about the "just powers" of the government coming from the "consent of the governed" was cast aside due to the specter of economic collapse and financial ruin, thus the war came.

Final Thoughts

By Barry Lee Clark

There is not a single word written on a single page of this work about overthrowing a government, rebellion or starting a war. Contrary to the image that revisionist and reconstructionist have tried to paint of the idea and notion of secession, it remains what it has always been, a form of political expression, a political theory. In the modern vernacular anyone that supports secession as a political theory is nothing more than a neo-Confederate bent on bringing back the Old South. Mr. Kirkpatrick Sale and the Middlebury Institute and the work they have done with and assortment of groups ought to disprove that idea all together. As a viable political theory, secession is a tool that ought to be retained and available to all peoples, in all places, as a means to express their political will, regardless of their political leaning.

On the practical side of the argument, secession remains merely a political theory (discounted by those that find it inconvenient). For those that worry that even talking of secession is anything but negative terms will lead to a reestablishment of The Confederacy there is no need for concern. In 1930 twelve Southerners wrote a prophetic book, *I'll Take My Stand*, in which they encouraged Southerners to take stock of their cultural, artistic and familial heritage and warned that Southerners, as a people, would disappear from the face of the Earth if they continued down the path of progressivism, industrialism and consumerism the writer say as destroyers of the Southern nation and people. I wrote an essay in 2012 discussion my view of how far down the prophetic path predicted in 1930 we have come. My conclusion is that Southerners are no longer a distinguishable people, no longer a nation. [81]

Secession, even if accepted as a valid political theory and a right requires, I believe, a people to create a nation. Therefore, the apparent fear that acknowledging the truths revealed in the essays within this work might lead to the reemergence of an "evil Confederacy" are misplaced at best, and inanely stupid and dishonest at worst.

Secession Quotes as parting thoughts:

"Any people anywhere, being inclined and having the power, have the right to rise up and shake off the existing government, and form a new one that suits them better. This is a most valuable, a most sacred right – a right which we hope and believe is to liberate the world. Nor is this right confined to cases in which the whole people of an existing government may choose to exercise it. Any portion of such people, that can, may revolutionize, and make their own of so much of the territory as they inhabit." – Abraham Lincoln, (speech in Congress January 1848)

"A nation, therefore, has no right to say to a province: You belong to me, I want to take you. A province consists of its inhabitants. If anybody has a right to be heard in this case it is these inhabitants." - Ludwig Von Mises. Omnipotent Government, p.90
"This and no other is the root from which a tyrant springs; when he first appears he is a protector." – Plato (circa 400 B.C.)

"When all government, in little as in great things, shall be drawn to Washington as the Center of all power, it will render powerless the checks provided of one government on another and will become as venal and oppressive as the government from which we separated." – Thomas Jefferson

"The constitution is not an instrument for the government to restrain the people, it is an instrument for the people to restrain the government - lest it come to dominate our lives and interests."-Patrick Henry
"Only a despotic and imperial government can coerce seceding states" - William Seward

US Secretary of State under Abraham Lincoln in 10 April 1861 to Charles Francis Adams, Minister to the Court of St. James (Britain)

"We do heartily accept this doctrine, believing it intrinsically sound, beneficent, and one that, universally accepted, is calculated to prevent the shedding of seas of human blood. And, if it justified the secession from the British Empire of Three Millions of colonists in 1776, we do not see why it would not justify the secession of Five Millions of Southrons from the Federal Union in 1861." - The New-York Daily Tribune, December 17, 1860

"The consolidation of the states into one vast republic, sure to be aggressive abroad and despotic at home, will be the certain precursor of that ruin of all that has proceeded it." - Robert E. Lee to Lord Acton December 15, 1866

"We dissent . . . because the powers vested in Congress by this constitution, must necessarily annihilate and absorb the legislative, executive, and judicial powers of he several states, and produce from their ruins one consolidated government, which from the nature of things will be an iron handed despotism, as nothing short of the supremacy of despotic sway could connect and govern these United States under one government. . . . [I]t would . . . produce a despotism, and that not by the usual gradations, but with the celerity that has hitherto only attended revolutions effected by the sword." (The Address and Reasons of Dissent of the Minority of the Convention of Pennsylvania to their Constituents, December 18, 1787), in R. Ketchum, ed., The Anti-Federalist Papers, pp. 237-256).

Appendix

Executive Usurpation [82]

James A. Bayard

Mr. President, during the special session of the Senate in March last, when seven States had withdrawn, by the action of their people, from the Federal Union, disclaimed all allegiance to the Government, and organized a separate common government, I took occasion, before the public mind had become excited, to express fully my views of the structure of our Government, and the unhappy condition of the country; and also to indicate the course of action which I believed most conducive to our happiness and prosperity in the future. I then thought, after the most anxious and gravest consideration, and actuated by no earthly motive but the good of my country, that the only alternative which remained was an assent to the revolution by which the Gulf States had left us, or civil war. That though the secession of a State was an act of revolution, it was an event not provided for by the Constitution, and could only be met by war or peace. That the power to coerce a State by the General Government by arms, having been expressly refused by the framers of the Constitution, we had no other resource left but war against them for a breach of the compact upon which the Federal Government is founded, or peace and the recognition of the common government which they had organized.

I did not doubt that the right of judgment as to peace or war-rested in Congress; but I was unable to see how any plea of executing the laws or retaking the public property justified the use of the. military power as a primary power, for that purpose, within the intent of the Constitution and the powers conferred by it on Congress or the Executive. Believing, also, that the withdrawal of those States did not subvert our Government, but left us a great and powerful nation, I thought a peaceful separation preferable to what I consider the greatest curse which the providence of God can inflict upon a nation—civil war. I also indulged the hope, and now believe that hope would have been realized, that by conciliation those States might be restored to the Union, and expressed the opinion that an attempt at coercion would drive other States out of the Confederacy; and in this, at least, subsequent events have shown that I was not in error. The Executive, as I deem most unfortunately, adopted the policy of coercion, and collision followed. An appeal by proclamation was made to the people for volunteers, which, involved of necessity coercion by arms and war, and four more States withdrew from the Union, and joined the Confederate States. The convention of Virginia had shown by repeated votes that a majority exceeding seventy existed in that body deeply attached to the Union, anxious to retain the State in the Union, and to settle the causes of difficulty which had arisen among us. On the President's proclamation, that convention seceded from the Union, and by an overwhelming majority of the people of Virginia their action has been ratified. Tennessee, which a brief time before had refused by thirty thousand majority to call a contention, immediately, by the action of her Legislature, left the Union, and her people ratified the act by sixty thousand majority. North Carolina withdrew with entire unanimity, though she had voted down a convention a short time before; and Arkansas, which had from her love to the Union postponed any consideration of the question of secession till the fall; in order that so eventful a matter should be fully discussed before her people, and its effects gravely weighed before determination, also left us, as consequent upon the proclamation.

Much as I deplored the loss of the Gulf States, I was then willing, to use the language of Burke, in 1777, in relation to our own Revolution:

"To part with them as a limb, but as a limb to save the body; and I would have parted with more, if more had been necessary; anything rather than a fruitless, hopeless, unnatural civil war."

Sir, I am as deeply attached to the Union as any man who claims a seat in this body. I would have saved it in its integrity by conciliation and compromise; and it is my consolation that, in my past life, no word or act of mine ever encouraged a sectional feeling among my countrymen. Nay, more, if any sacrifice on my part, involving property or even life itself, could now end this unhappy struggle, and restore and preserve the Union, with the fraternal feeling and national sentiment in which it was founded by our forefathers, that sacrifice would be readily and cheerfully made. I could leave no richer or prouder inheritance to my children than the reflection that their father, had sacrificed himself for the prosperity and welfare of his country.

But the passions of the nation have become excited, and the cry now is, "unconditional submission and the crushing out of rebellion," without the first step having been taken for the purpose, of conciliation. States are to be reduced to provinces, and the military power to become the dominant power in a representative republic. Even a servile insurrection is threatened, should it prove necessary, for the purpose of conquest and subjugation.

"Unconditional submission, and the crushing out of rebellion" was the language of the Crown and ministers of Great Britain in the struggle in which our ancestors achieved our liberties. No terms should be offered to armed rebels; the sword and the bayonet were the only admissible arguments. The Government was to be strengthened, and the Colonies to be subdued. The habeas corpus act was suspended in America and on the high seas, and those who sailed under letters of marque issued by the United States Congress were denounced as pirates. Let me read the answer to this course of policy of Mr. Burke, which embodies the general sentiment of the greatest statesmen and truest patriots of England in that day. I read from his letter to the sheriffs of Bristol, in April, 1777, less than a year after our independence had been declared; and for its general truths, as applicable to the present struggle, the whole letter might be read with profit by every well-wisher of his country: "It is said that, being at war with the colonies, whatever our sentiments might have been before, ail ties between us are now dissolved; and all the policy we have left is to strengthen the hands of the Government to reduce them. On the principle of this argument, the more mischief we suffer from. any administration, the more our trust in it is to be confirmed. Let them but once get us into a war, and then their power fs safe, and an act of oblivion is passed for all their misconduct. But is it true that Government is always to be strengthened with the instruments of war, but never furnished with the means of peace? In former times, ministers, I allow, have been sometimes driven by the popular voice to assert by arms the national honor against foreign powers. But the wisdom of the nation has been far more clear when those ministers have been compelled to consult its interests by treaty." Further: "This mode of yielding would, it is said, give way to independency without a war. But if it had this effect, I confess that I should prefer independency without war to independency with it; and I have so much trust in the inclinations and prejudices of mankind, and so little in anything else, that I should expect ten times more benefit to this kingdom." The United States, Mr. President—

"from the affection of America,"—
The South—
"though under a separate establishment, than from her perfect submission to the Crown and parliament"—
The Federal Government—
"accompanied with her terror, disgust, and abhorrence. "Bodies tied together by so unnatural a bond of union as mutual hatred, are only connected to their ruin."

Could we, Mr. President, if after a desolating war we succeeded in subjugating the South, bind her to us by any other bonds of union than mutual hatred, and is it not true that such a bond of union would involve the ruin of both the North and the South?

It has been said that if we let these States go in peace we yield to the right of secession at will by a State, and that such a principle will lead to the entire disintegration of the Union. But we do not yield to the right of secession by recognizing revolution. I admit that were a single State to secede—even a large State—restriction and coercion, (not by arms,) coupled with conciliation, might well be used, and would be successful in restoring her. Such was the course of our ancestors in the adoption of the Constitution to the small State of Rhode Island and the larger State of North Carolina, one of which remained out of the Union after the organization of the Federal Government for one year, and the other a year and a half. I admit, also, that secession is revolution, and that we have the right of war in such a case, if Congress so decides. But the object of the war ought to be the restoration of the State to the Union, and, as against a single State, the menace of war would in all probability, from the superior power of the Federal Government, effect its object without bloodshed.

I dismiss, therefore, all apprehensions from my mind arising from the recognition of a revolution inaugurated and carried on by a large section of the country by the collective action of its people, as conceding the right of secession or leading to the future disintegration of the Union. Sir, in the Revolution of 1776, Massachusetts was the colony that first embarked in resistance to the mother country. Does any gentleman suppose that revolutions must not be dealt with according to their magnitude? Can there be a doubt that the mistake which Great Britain made then, was in attributing the spirit of resistance to the leaders alone, when the hearts of the people were in the contest? Governor Gage issued his proclamation in Boston, in which he offered to all the inhabitants of the colony entire protection and amnesty, with the exception of John Hancock and Samuel Adams, if they would lay down their arms and submit to the Government; but the offer was of no avail. Does any gentleman suppose that the colony of Massachusetts alone could have resisted the power of the British Government, unless the sympathies of the people of the other colonies had been enlisted, and they had made common cause with her? Having a common interest, they united to resist an exercise of power which, if submitted to by one colony, would in the end be crushing to the liberties of all. Had those ministers not been blind to the general sentiment of the people of the colonies, they would not have held and acted upon the mistaken idea which is now so rife in relation to the seceding States, that it was the leaders alone, and not the people, whose hearts were in the cause, and Great Britain would probably in the first instance, have parted with her colonies in peace, or retained her general authority by concessions, saving herself a debt of more than a thousand million dollars, and also carrying on with them a commercial intercourse far more profitable to her than would have existed if the powers which she claimed over an unwilling people had been enforced by subjugation. Revolution by a large section of country, composed of eleven States, with singular unanimity on the part of their people, cannot be met by war, if the object be the restoration of the Union and its preservation as a representative republic.

Sir, on this subject let me show you what are not merely my opinions of the impracticability of a single republic over so extensive a country as ours without the existence of the internal governments of separate independent States, bound together by one common government over communities separate among themselves and constituting us a nation as regards the world at large; but the opinions universally entertained at the time the convention sat which framed the Federal Constitution. No abler man, with rare exceptions, at least, if any, than Mr. Wilson, of Pennsylvania, was found in that convention. His name appeared as an active participator in all its debates. He was one of the framers of the Constitution, peculiarly entitled to our gratitude, and one of its most ardent supporters, both in its original formation and in its adoption by his own State. I read from a speech which he made in favor of the adoption of the Constitution by the people of Pennsylvania, in the convention of that State, and I read it in order to show the danger of consolidation into a single government, which is inevitably incident to the subjugation of the Southern States by the military power:
"The United States may adopt any one of four different systems. They may become consolidated into one Government, in which the separate existence of the States shall be entirely absolved."

They may reject any plan of union or association, and act as separate and unconnected States. They may form two or more confederacies. They may unite in one federal republic. Which of these systems ought to have been formed by the convention? To support with vigor a single Government over the whole extent of the United States would demand a system of the most unqualified and most unremitted despotism. Such a number of separate States, contiguous in situation, unconnected and disunited in government, would be at one time the prey of foreign force, foreign influence, and foreign intrigues, at another the victims of mutual rage, rancor, and revenge. Neither of these systems found advocates in the late convention. I presume they will not find advocates in this."

After, discussing .the relative merits of a union of two or more republics, or into one, he speaks of "the remaining system," which was' adopted, "as a union of them into one confederate republic." No man can doubt that the words "confederate" and "federal" are synonymous, and when applied to this republic, or any other, imply, from the force of the words, a common government over separate independent communities.

I have read it, sir, to warn gentlemen that the system of government adopted in 1787 is inconsistent with the prosecution of war for the subjection of the South; and yet you cannot execute the laws, as you claim to do, within the Confederate States without their entire conquest and subjugation. You must, if successful, convert, and it has been threatened by many leading papers, and by at least one leading member of the administration, that you will convert this Government into a single Government, and absolve all State lines. In answer to such a purpose, and as an all-sufficient objection to it, I give you the great general truth enunciated by Mr. Wilson, that a government of that kind, to exist over the extent of this country, must be "a system of the most unqualified and unremitting despotism."

Sir, I would preserve the Union. Why? To preserve the liberties of my country. If the Union is to be made the means of prostrating those liberties, then it is far better that the Union should be abandoned than that free institutions should be abolished. I value and cherish it, not merely because it gives us a powerful Government, but because its power secures and protects the individual liberty of the citizen, and because the Union, under a Federal Constitution, will perpetuate republican institutions, and preserve self-government by the people.

By war you may subjugate and devastate the Southern States; but the large army you must permanently maintain to keep them in subjection will inevitably, in the end, subvert our own institutions and convert a republic into an autocracy. It is easier to organize than to disband a large army; and more difficult still to disband a dictator when you have yielded to him the power of the sword and the purse and subordinated the civil to the military power.

But have Senators reflected on the effects of civil war upon the character and habits of the people, and its demoralizing influences? Let me give you the portraiture of those effects and influences, in the language of the same great statesman; because the truth is general and as applicable to our times as to the day in which he lived. "Civil wars," said Mr. Burke— "Civil wars strike deepest of all into the manners of the people. They vitiate their politics; they corrupt their morals; they pervert even the natural taste and relish of equity and justice. By teaching us to consider our fellow-citizens in a hostile light, the whole body of our nation becomes gradually less dear to us. The very names of affection and kindred which were the bonds of charity whilst we agreed become new incentives to hatred and rage when the communion of our country is dissolved. We may flatter ourselves that we shall not fall into this misfortune ; but we have no charter of exemption that I know of from the ordinary frailties of our nature."

If the language of the statesman will not convince you, take .the corroboration in the experience of the soldier: "It has been my fortune to have seen much of war, more than most, men. I have been constantly engaged in the active duties of the military profession from boyhood until I have grown gray. My life has been passed in familiarity with scenes of death and suffering. Circumstances have placed me in countries where the war was internal—between opposite parties in the same nation—and rather than a country I loved should be visited with the calamities which I have seen, with the unutterable horrors of civil war, I would run any risk, I would make any sacrifice, I would freely lay down my life. There is nothing which destroys property and prosperity and demoralizes character to the extent which civil war does. By it the hand of man is raised against his neighbor, against his brother, against his father; the servant betrays his master, and the master ruin his servant."

Such was the experience of the great Duke of Wellington, and I pray God we may profit by that experience before it is too late. Sir, it may be that I have a more vivid imagination, or that my nerves are less firm than those of my brother Senators; but I confess, that when I think of the blood that must flow in this contest, this unnatural contest, of the devastation that must ensue, of the human lives that must be sacrificed, a shudder runs through my frame, and my heart sickens with despair. I am for peace, an armistice and negotiation, whether by a general convention or by treaty, or in any other mode; I care not for the mode, if civil war can be terminated, and peace come to my country. I would receive the proposals of those who have at least been once our brethren. I would yield nothing which I thought degraded the United States, or subverted our form of government; but I would, by compromise, restore them to the Union if possible. If that were impracticable, I would part with them in peace, on a just and equitable settlement. We know that they claim their independence, and offer to account for all the public property which they have taken; that they have neither invaded us, nor expressed any intention to invade us, but claim their own right of self-government, founded on "the consent of the governed." If their terms of settlement be unjust, reject them, and continue the war until they submit to just terms and an equitable adjustment. But you must receive their offers before you can decide on their admissibility, unless, indeed, unconditional submission be, like the demand of Great Britain from our ancestors, your absolute determination. Those ancestors owed allegiance to the crown of England, and rebelled; the government of England said without cause. Eleven States have revolted by the collective action of their people against the Federal Government, and you say without cause. Admitting that they have exaggerated their causes of complaint; admitting that they were precipitate in their action, and that their sense of insecurity to their property and social institutions under the Federal Government has been entirely over-estimated; yet I tell you that it is a truth which the records of history will not gainsay, that "such

an event as the disaffection and revolt of a whole people
never took place without some considerable errors of
conduct observed towards them."

Senators, I am well aware that the administration and
an overwhelming majority of Congress do not and will
not assent to my views; that you regard force and war
as the true and only mode of preserving the Union,
whilst I have a confident belief that the continuance of
war will inevitably subvert the republic, and substitute a
military government for civil liberty and a government of
laws. I am satisfied that you have determined on war. I
impugn no man's motives, though I dissent from your
judgment, and condemn your policy of war. Resistance,
however, to the will of such a majority, I know to be
futile and hopeless, and I mean to embark in no factious
opposition to your practical measures; your practical
legislation, therefore, has met, and will meet, no cavils
or objections from me; except, indeed, bills should be
introduced, palpably violating the Constitution of my
country. "With you rests the responsibility and as I
cannot conscientiously support a course of action which
is against my conviction, nor wisely contend with a
majority which I know to be irresistible, I shall await that
change in public sentiment which I feel confident will
take place, when the hour of passionate excitement has
passed, and the blighting influences of civil war have
awakened what Fisher Ames well called "the second
sober thought of the people."

Much as I dissent from the President's message in its
mode of stating facts, its arguments, and its omissions, I
forbear even a single comment, open as I believe it to
just criticism. I leave that task to others, by whom, in
my opinion, it has been well performed. But I have some
hope, some faint hope, that you may be induced to
refrain from passing the resolution now before the
Senate, which involves no practical legislation, unless
indeed there is an intent—which I do not suppose—to
suspend, by indirection, the writ of habeas corpus in the
future. I proceed now to the consideration of the
resolution.

The joint resolution imports not merely an approval of the acts of the President, but a declaration that all the acts enumerated in the preamble are to be in all respects legal and valid, to the same intent and with the same effect as if they had been issued and done under the previous express authority and direction of the Congress of the United States. As regards four of those acts, it would be very immaterial whether you passed this resolution or not; as regards the other two, it is of the last importance to the liberty of every man in the United States that you should not pass it.

The preamble recites the act of the President in calling volunteers into the service on the 15th of April; to the act of blockade of certain ports on the 19th of April, and of other ports on the 27th of April, by executive authority, when no law authorized the executive to exert such a power. The fourth act recited relates to the suspension of the writ of habeas corpus, and the delegation of the power to suspend it to a subordinate officer under the President; the fifth to the proclamation increasing the army of the United States, and calling additional volunteers into service; and the sixth to a further suspension of the habeas corpus act. The first three and the fifth are all provided for by laws which you have passed, or will pass at this session. You have provided for the volunteers that were called out on the 15th of April. That sanctions the act, as far as you can sanction it, and provides for the payment of the men. I do not dispute your right to do that. You have passed a bill to authorize a blockade of the ports of certain States in the future; and though on your theory, I consider that Congress has no authority to institute or authorize such a blockade, yet, on mine, I do not deny the constitutionality of the act, if it is passed by virtue of the war-making power, for that is in the absolute discretion of Congress. And , what is blockade but a belligerent right? Whoever heard of it under any other aspect, or by any other name? If you are at war, you can declare a blockade; and to be at war, it is not necessary that you should formally declare war against those States; but if by your acts you recognize a state of war with them, beyond all question war exists as between these United States and the Confederate States. You have done so by many acts; you will do so by more. I do not, therefore, dispute your right of blockade, though I deny that within the intent of the Constitution, you could blockade a port of a State still in the Union in consistence with that provision of the Constitution which inhibits Congress from giving a preference to the ports of one State over those of another. I do not mean to enter into that argument, because I admit your authority under the war power, and I know that we are now in a state of civil war; and you have actually recognized a war between these eleven States and the United States Government, though you have not formally declared `it.

Mr. President, what is the rule as among nations? During our last war with Great Britain, she had possession of a portion of our territory in the State of Maine, Eastport and the surrounding country. The courts of the United States decided that the laws of the United States were suspended within that territory in the possession of a foreign enemy during the time that it was so in their actual possession; and precisely the same principle applies to civil war that the laws of the United States are suspended where the possession is in the party at war with the Government—call them by what name you please— rebels, revolutionists, or enemies. The doctrine in England always was, that the laws were suspended, the habeas carpus act and all, within that portion of the territory where the king's court could not be opened. I do not deny that the President may exercise military powers there;' but I deny that in the States which belong to the Union, in which the courts are open, in which justice can be administered between man and man, the military can be made predominant over the civil power, either by Congress or by the President, without a gross violation of the Constitution.

I come next to the question of the army. No man could pretend to affirm that the President had authority to, increase the army of the United States without a precedent law. No one for a moment could affirm that the power to raise and increase the army is not vested in Congress. You have approved the increase in the only mode in which you can legitimately sanction such an act. You have approved it by passing a bill providing for the organization of that army, and for the present and future pay of that army. I do not deny your right to do that. The-measure is perfectly legitimate when you have determined on war, and if you choose to sanction the conduct of the President by appropriate legislation, I shall offer no vain opposition to your measures, because I differ with your policy, when I find the majority here determined on that policy.

But, sir, the suspension of the writ of habeas corpus has a very different aspect if approved by Congress. If you think that the state of the country and the public exigency require that the writ of habeas corpus should be suspended, do it openly in the face of the country; do it by your legislation; but do not attempt to do it indirectly; do not an act which you will hereafter regret, which will strike the most fatal blow at the liberties of this country which has ever yet been stricken, by the affirmation of the power in a President of the United States—a single man—to suspend the writ of habeas corpus whenever in his discretion he may think such such suspension advisable. Such is the effect of your resolution. The resolution is improper, because, if you think the writ ought to be suspended, you can suspend it by your own action. You have a right, under that action, to designate the States in which it which it shall be suspended, and to limit the time for which it shall be suspended. That is the course which has always been adopted in Great Britain for the last two hundred years, whenever it was necessary under any emergency to suspend the writ of habeas corpus, the great writ of right, which is the sole remedy of the subject to secure his right of personal liberty and personal freedom—which is the sole remedy for freedom of the citizen here. It has been done by act of Parliament always; and no king of England in two hundred years past has ever ventured to suspend the writ of habeas corpus, though, until the judiciary became independent of the Crown, his judges sometimes evaded the issuance of the writ. Still less did any king of England ever claim the power of delegating such a high discretionary authority to any subordinate officer. Sir, the power is incapable of delegation, whether it is in the President of the United States or in the Congress of the United States; and yet the President of the United States, according to his order as given, and I believe correctly given, in the newspapers, though I have not seen it elsewhere, and according to the recital of this resolution, did not himself decide that the state and condition of any part of the country required that the writ should be suspended, and the remedy for the civil liberty of the citizen thrown aside, but delegated the right of decision upon the political exigency which might justify and require the suspension of the sole remedy for the liberty of every citizen of the United States to military and subordinate officers. If the right exists in him, he had no power of delegation. If the right exists in us, it was palpable usurpation; and yet you propose, not only to approve, but to affirm the validity of an act directly in the face of the Federal Constitution.

The President in his message claims that the power is vested in him as the executive, to suspend the writ of habeas corpus in his discretion. In the message, he alluded to the opinion of the Attorney General which has since been furnished to Congress. In that opinion the Attorney General, by an argument the most extraordinary which ever came from the pen of a lawyer, attempts to sustain the same doctrine. If the Congress of the United States not only approves the act but affirms its validity and legality, I ask where is our Government? The whole power of the purse and the sword you have given to him; the unlimited command of men and money. You have voted $500,000,000 and five hundred thousand men; and you now, by the indirect action of affirming an unconstitutional act, propose to yield to him the right to arrest any citizen of these free United States on suspicion, without proof of guilt, and without process of law.

Sir, can it be that the Senate will pass such a resolution as this without striking out these clauses, at least? Strike them out, and I care little for the resolution. In the case of blockade, I am willing to leave it to the courts. You cannot legalize a past act by your now determination, where it involves a forfeiture; and therefore, if the President had no right to declare a blockade—if a vessel was intercepted before your law passes, and the case comes before the courts— the courts will decide, without reference to your resolution, whether the President had authority to institute the blockade; for if he had not, of course there could be no forfeiture under it. To pass such a law and make it retroactive, is clearly to pass an ex post facto law. It involves a penalty arising out of an act made criminal, by subsequent legislation, which was not criminal or prohibited by the law at the time when the act was done; that is, the attempt of any vessel to sail from or enter into any of the ports of the seceded States. On what principle can you, in the face of the Constitution, affirm by legislation such action as that? You are not vested with judicial power; the judicial power is, by the Constitution, given to the Supreme Court and the subordinate courts that you have established. If you arrogate to yourselves judicial powers, you are departing plainly from the mandate of the constitution; and you are destroying the Government, which is made a free Government by a division of the powers of government between separate and co-ordinate departments—the judiciary being by far the weakest of them all. But if, in addition to sanctioning a blockade instituted without color of law, the Congress of the United States chooses to vest in the President, by indirect action, judicial power to determine when the citizen's liberty shall be taken from him for any extent of time, at his discretion, it is perfectly certain that you are establishing a mere absolutism, and that you have abandoned your form of government altogether.

Sir, I do not propose to enter into any long discussion about this writ of habeas corpus. The decision of the Supreme Court of the United States, (which, differing from the learned Attorney General, I consider does settle principles and not merely decide cases,) made more than fifty years ago, held that the suspension of the writ was a legislative and not an executive power; and I consider the decision of the Chief Justice in the case of Merryman so utterably unanswerable, that it would be an idle attempt on my part to expect to reach or to change the opinions of a man who could read it and remain unconvinced. It has gone to the people of the country. I think the people of the country will appreciate the force and power of the opinion when the time of excitement has passed; and I trust it is passing rapidly.

But, sir, there are some things connected with this writ that it is necessary I should advert to. My objection relates to your affirmance of the validity of the power of the President to suspend the writ of habeas corpus whenever, in his discretion, he thinks the circumstances justify it; that he is to be the judge of the political exigency which requires the suspension of the writ. Such is his claim. This resolution, if passed, affirms that claim, and approves and declares the suspension of the writ to be a power vested in the executive and capable of delegation. The language of your resolution is, that the suspension is declared to be "in all respects legal and valid," and you embody in that resolution no denial of the claim of power; and where, then, stand the people of the United States in the future? A single man becomes a despot; he has the power of the purse and the sword, and you give him the absolute control over the liberty of every citizen in the United States, to be exercised by himself or any subordinate officer to whom he may see fit to confide its exercise, in the absolute discretion of either the President or the subordinate.

The Attorney General has given an opinion in support of this power in the executive; and I purpose commenting on, at most, two of his conclusions. First, let me make a short statement in reference to the writ of habeas corpus, and read one or two authorities in connection with it. The clause of the Constitution which restricts the suspension of the writ of habeas corpus, except in cases of rebellion or invasion, merely secures the remedy of the citizens against illegal imprisonment, and the only remedy which the laws provide. The right to liberty, and freedom from imprisonment, without due process of law, is secured by the Constitution of the United States beyond your power to violate, as well as beyond the power of the President, unless you mean to trample upon that Constitution. What is the language of the fifth article of the amendments to the Constitution? That no person shall "be compelled, in any criminal case, to be a witness against himself, nor be deprived of life, liberty," or property, without due process of law." If you arrest him and confine him, do you not deprive him of liberty? Is it by "due process of law," if the arrest is made by the military power without oath, without judicial investigation, without evidence of probable cause founded upon oath? The words "due process of law," have their own settled meaning, which no lawyer has ever doubted. They come from Magna Charta, "the law of the land," and "due process of law" meaning one and the same thing. If you want the exposition of their meaning, you have but to turn to Coke's Second Institute in order to find it. Magna Charta restricted the power of the crown, because the contest then was between the crown and the barons, representing themselves and the people of England; but in our country, and in all the States, as well as in the Federal Constitution, the restriction and the protection it secures to the liberty of every citizen, applies to all departments of the Government—the legislature, the executive, or the judiciary. A man's right to his personal liberty, unless on a warrant issued for a civil debt, or on due process of law for a criminal charge founded on probable cause, substantiated by oath, is secured in the constitution of every State of this Union, and in the Constitution of the

United States; and Congress has no power of suspending the right, even in case of rebellion, insurrection, or war, though it may suspend the remedy by habeas corpus, in cases when, from rebellion or invasion, the public safety requires such suspension. The only exception to the invasion of the citizen's right of liberty, without due process of law, is "in cases arising in the land and naval forces, or in the militia, when in actual service in time of war or public danger." I admit that in those States in which by war the laws are suspended, the right and the remedy are suspended, and you may exercise in them the rights of a belligerent; but in the States in the Union, if the habeas corpus act were suspended by Congress, the President would have no right to arrest by military power. He could only lawfully arrest the citizen not found in arms against the Government by the civil power, and for probable cause of guilt, founded upon oath. It is true, though, that if you take away the only remedy which the law gives for a judicial investigation, if the arrest is made, the party is entirely helpless; and therefore it is that the suspension, of the remedy has been often confounded with the suspension of the right. The right stands beyond your power, without a violation of the Constitution. The remedy—and the only remedy—which secures the right, you may suspend in certain conditions, of the country, where the public safety requires it; but the discretion to suspend is vested in Congress, and riot in the executive branch of the Government.

We have derived this remedy by habeas corpus from the common law. We have also derived the great principle that the citizen shall not be deprived of his personal liberty, except by "due process of law" from the common law, and have incorporated it into our fundamental law, as the inviolate right of every American citizen. Let us recur to the law as it existed in England when these States were colonies, for by such reference only can we reach a correct construction of the intent with which these clauses in relation to "due process of law" and the writ of habeas corpus were inserted in the Constitution.

No one doubts that by the law of England since Magna Charta, if not before, no subject could be deprived of his liberty without "due process of law," and was entitled of right to the writ of habeas corpus for the purpose of a judicial investigation into the cause of his confinement. Yet in practice the crown frequently invaded the personal liberty of the subject, and disregarded the writ, and there was a long struggle between the Commons and the crown for this great remedy, because without the remedy the right was a nullity, and the subject was at the mercy of the crown; and his liberty could be invaded at pleasure, without "due process of law," by arbitrary and unlawful arrest and confinement.

To show the character of this writ, and demonstrate that the authority to suspend it was always a legislative and not an executive power, I will read from an entry on the Commons' Journal, made on the 3d of April, 1628, during the reign of the Stuarts, in which the law is declared, while the contest for the liberty of the subject against arbitrary arrest by the crown was still in progress between the Commons of England and, the crown:

"Resolved upon question, That the writ of habeas corpus may not be denied, but ought to be granted to every man that is committed or detained in prison, or otherwise restrained, though it be by the command of the king, the privy council, or any other, he praying the same—without one negative."

That is the resolution of the British House of Commons without dissent in 1628. I find, further, on turning to the Lords' Journal in February 1704, privileged as they were and hereditary as was their rank, that they valued the civil liberty of their countrymen:

"Resolved, That every Englishman who is imprisoned by any authority whatsoever, has an undoubted, right, by his agents or friends, to apply for and obtain a writ of habeas corpus, in order to procure his liberty, by due course of law."

Again, sir, on a representation made to the crown on the 15th of March, 1704, by the Lords, it is said with great distinctness:

"It has been allowed, by the known common law, it is the right of every subject under restraint, upon demand, to have the writ of habeas corpus, and thereupon to be brought before some proper court, where it may be examined whether he be detained for a lawful cause."

Such was the law of England long before our Revolution, when we were colonies of England; such is the principle that was meant to be embodied in the Constitution of the United States by that restriction against the suspension of the writ of habeas corpus—a restriction, not on the power of the President, for he never had it; but an exception to the powers granted to Congress; and the effect is to make it mandatory on Congress to pass a law providing for the issuance of the writ by the judiciary, because the issuing of the writ and the execution of the writ are judicial matters from beginning to end, and always have been. It belongs to that department of our government in which the Constitution vests the judicial power of the country. Congress have the right to suspend it in certain cases, but that very right of suspension renders it compulsory on them, if they do not mean to violate the Constitution, to provide by law, in such courts as they see fit to establish, the power and impose the duty to issue and enforce this great writ. They did make such provision by law, in 1789, among the first acts after the organization of the Government under the Constitution. The fourteenth and fifteenth sections of the judiciary act give to the Supreme Court and its judges, in all cases of commitment, the power, and impose the duty, to inquire into the cause of commitment, by and through the writ of habeas corpus. The power is there by law, and the law has not been suspended. On what principle is it that any President of the United States can suspend or disobey a law of the United States? The great doctrine proclaimed has been that it was his duty to execute the laws in the seceding States. Is he to execute the laws by violating the laws, as a first step of action, in the States which have not seceded? What power has the President of the United States to suspend a law of the land? What king of England can do it, unless it is expressed in the law itself that he has such discretionary power? No such discretion is given, and the fourteenth and fifteenth sections of your judiciary act require the court to issue this writ, on application, whenever a party is confined, and determine whether the commitment is legal. If the imprisonment is not lawful, it is the duty of the court or judge to discharge him.

If Congress mean to affirm that this power is in the President of the United States, I want it to go forth to this nation that they have virtually suspended the writ of habeas corpus, not by law, but by affirmative resolution, exercising a judicial authority which is not vested in them—an affirmation declaring that the President, in this country, can trespass upon the liberty of the citizen in a manner which would have cost any king of England his crown for the last two hundred years, if he had dared to exercise such a power.

I submit, therefore, that if the President had the power, being the exercise of a high discretion founded upon the condition of the nation, of course it would be incapable of delegation. If, as I believe, the power exists in Congress, neither can Congress delegate it. If the exigencies of this country and the public safety, in your opinion, require that you should now suspend the habeas corpus act, you may, as they do in England, describe the States or parts of States into which the writ shall not run during the time limited in the law. In England, I can find not a single instance on record where the suspension has ever been for more than one year. During the contest with her colonies, the attempt was made to suspend the writ of habeas corpus by legislation, with provisions which would have involved the suspension in England as well as here; but the opposition, after discussing the question, forced the ministers to abandon that portion of the bill, because they found that the majority of the lawyers supporting them were opposed to so extended a suspension. The bill was, therefore, modified so as to suspend the writ in the rebellious colonies and on the high seas; that is, they authorized the apprehension of persons on suspicion in the rebellious colonies and on the high seas, and their confinement, at the discretion of the king, until the 1st of January, 1778, not quite a year from the passage of the bill. Here it is not the passage of a bill; it is not the exercise of a high discretion where, after full consideration, you decide that the public safety requires this great remedy—which is the only remedy to preserve the liberty of the citizen—shall be suspended, and where and for what length of time it shall be suspended; but you affirm an act of the President, done in his discretion, not in yours, in the past, which is clearly unconstitutional, and which you have not the power to affirm. By affirming his act as he claims the power, you are virtually assenting, on the part of the legislature, to the claim of power on the part of the President; and thus the constitutional division of powers, which is the security of our Government as a free Government, is to be abandoned.

I shall read one or two extracts from judicial decisions to show the uniform construction by judicial exposition. There can be no question that, in the case of Bollman and Swartout, the Supreme Court decided, in distinct terms, that the power was in the legislature, and the legislature not having exercised any power to suspend the writ, even though insurrection existed, the court were bound to execute the law, and the evidence not being sufficient, they discharged the prisoners. They positively affirmed the power to be in the legislature ; and I had never heard, until the claim was made by the present Executive, of a solitary lawyer in the United States who ventured to doubt that the power was in Congress, and not in the President. In my judgment, a received construction of more than half a century, and a settled opinion of the profession, is always strong evidence of what the law really is.

The essential requisites for the lawful deprivation of the liberty of the citizen, are clearly and distinctly stated by the Supreme Court ex parte Buford, 3 Cranch, 451: "The judges of the court are unanimously of opinion that the warrant of commitment was illegal for the want of stating some good cause certain, supported by oath."

Where, let me ask, would be the liberty of the citizen, if the President can arrest at his discretion, and refuse to obey the writ of habeas corpus? Who is to decide whether there is a good cause certain, supported by oath?

It is absolute power. This is not a land of freedom and free institutions longer, when you have passed the resolution now before you.

The history of the habeas corpus act and its uses are well stated by the court in Watkins's case, Judge Marshall delivering the opinion, after stating the existence of the right at common law, says:

"The English judges being originally under the influence of the crown, neglected to issue this writ where the government entertained suspicions which would not be sustained by evidence; and the writ, when issued, was sometimes disregarded or evaded, and great individual oppression, in consequence of delays in bringing prisoners to trial. To remedy this evil, the celebrated habeas corpus act of 31 Charles II was enacted,".

That writ is the writ to which the court refer as securing to the people a judicial investigation; a writ of right which cannot, in the language of the House of Commons, two hundred and fifty years ago, be lawfully denied, though the arrest be by the command of the king. That right is to be abandoned in the republic of the United States, in the face of an express provision in the Constitution limiting your legislative powers, which prevents you from suspending it, except in a political exigency of invasion or rebellion, where the public safety requires it; of which you are to be the judges, and you alone. As to the meaning of the words "due process of law," as securing the rights of the citizen, I might refer to the opinion of a very able and distinguished judge of our own country, Mr. Justice Curtis, who, in a case which had no political bearings whatever, gave an exposition of the meaning of the words "law of the land," as existing in the constitution of Rhode Island, which is analogous to " due process of law" in our own Constitution.

Now, sir, let me notice for a moment some one or two of the somewhat singular views presented in the extraordinary opinion of the Attorney General. On page 5 of the opinion, he says:

"As to the first question, I am clearly of opinion that, in a time like the present when the very existence of the nation is assailed by a great and dangerous insurrection, the President has the lawful discretionary power to arrest and hold in custody persons known to have criminal intercourse with the insurgents or persons against whom there is probable cause for suspicion of such criminal complicity."

Here is a strange confusion of ideas. Every lawyer knows what "probable cause" means. Probable cause is something more than suspicion. It is a state of facts established upon oath, from which prima facie an inference of guilt can be rationally made. Whoever heard before of the term " probable cause" applied to mere suspicion, and not to the fact of guilt itself? There must be probable cause of guilt, and without that supported by oath, the court will discharge. There must also be authority for the arrest and commitment, or the court will discharge. If an offense be not charged, if there is no oath, or the oath does not show probable cause in support of the charges, as in the case of Swartout and Bollman, the court will discharge.

I might ask, further, in connection with this idea of probable cause, who is to decide it? What is the writ of habeas corpus? Is the President to execute it, because it is his duty to see that the laws are executed, or is it a judicial function? As I have read to you from the representations to the crown, made in 1704, in the British House of Lords, the party is to be taken before some court, in order that the matter may be inquired into, and if no probable cause of guilt is shown, he must be discharged. The matter is to be judicially inquired into, and by your Constitution the judicial power is vested in the courts of the United States, and not in the Executive. Who, then, is to determine the existence of probable cause? The tribunal, the authority to investigate and decide, seems to have been lost sight of by the learned Attorney General.

The learned Attorney General, after giving his opinion on the first point, assumes that the President has the legal discretionary power to arrest and imprison persons who are guilty of holding criminal intercourse with men in a great and dangerous insurrection, or persons suspected, "with probable cause," of such criminal complicity; and writes the words with marks of quotation to show that it is their legal meaning in which he uses them, "persons suspected with 'probable cause' of such complicity." Is there, I repeat, a lawyer in the land who does not know that probable cause is more than suspicion; that it implies prima facie evidence of guilt sufficient to hold the party for trial according to the law of the land, and that it stands contradistinguished from suspicion; that suspicion is no ground whatever for commitment upon arrest, unless sustained by an affidavit showing probable cause, not of suspicion, but of guilt? What is suspicion, Mr. President? Opinion, no more. Lord Bacon has well said: "Suspicions among thoughts are like bats among birds; they always fly in the dark." The suspicion of an administration, or of any man, can never be just ground for depriving a citizen of his liberty. In this country there must be probable cause of guilt, of offense against the laws, and shown by affidavit with sufficient certainty, in order to justify the incarceration of his person; and we have no free country when that ceases to be the law. Either enmity or timidity will suspect without cause, and power, too, will suspect where it wishes to crush an opponent. Unhappy, indeed, is the country where personal vengeance and political animosity can satiate itself by the imprisonment of its object upon suspicion.

Let me ask what constitutes the difference between the letter de cachet in the reign of Louis XIV and an arrest by the President of the United States, because he chooses to declare there is a state of insurrection, and, arrest at his discretion, or at the discretion of any subordinate officer, on suspicion of guilt? What constitutes the difference between the Bastile and Fort McHenry or any other fort of the United States? Louis XIV said "l'etat c'est moi" and he exercised the power of committing any subject of Prance to the Bastile to lay there in a dungeon for one year or ten, at his discretion. The individual might be forgotten, or he might be the subject of personal animosity, and it was so most frequently. But, at least, the act of arbitrary power had this restriction: it was always done under the immediate order of the sovereign. The President of the United States claims a similar power, not only to be exerted by himself, but by any subordinate to whom he chooses to delegate the authority; not only to suspend the habeas corpus act, but to arrest and incarcerate on suspicion at discretion; and the difference in the place of incarceration is, that Fort McHenry and your other forts may have no dungeons, but the restraint upon the liberty of the party is just as arbitrary and unlawful. The restraint, too, is claimed as discretionary in the duration of imprisonment. The punishment is the same, though it may not be characterized by the same brutality in the mode of confinement! If a man can be arrested and imprisoned at discretion, without proof of any criminal act—I mean prima facia proof, legal proof sufficient to hold him for trial—and can be held in prison for an indefinite time without being brought to trial, (which he can be if this great writ of right is suspended,) there is no remedy for him whatever. I ask, where is the liberty remaining to a single American citizen with such an exercise of authority by the President, sanctioned by the legislative power of the Union?

Mr. President, there is no other distinction between the condition of France under Louis XIV and present condition of these United States if this resolution be passed. The Bastile had its dungeons; the forts have none. Louis XIV alone issued his letters de cachet; but the President of the United States delegates a general power to one or ten different officers to arrest and imprison guiltless men, whenever the office chooses to suspect them of criminal complicity, and all this is to be sanctioned and continued in the face of a Constitution which we had supposed gave us, as citizens of a free country, free institutions, in contradistinction to the absolutism which reigned in France under Louis XIV.

Sir, there are other singular dicta, shall I call them, or propositions contained in this opinion, and it will be a celebrated opinion hereafter of the learned Attorney General. He even undertakes, from the form of the oath, to infer the grant of additional powers to the Executive —a singular inference indeed for a lawyer to draw in reference to a written Constitution and frame of government consisting of specially delegated powers. If the proposition were correct, inasmuch as the oath which is administered to us and to the judges of the Supreme Court is one and the same—that is, to support the Constitution of the United States—it would be difficult to define and distinguish our respective powers. There is, at least, the merit of novelty in the idea, that the powers granted under a written instrument are to be either enlarged or decreased by the mere form of the oath to be administered to the party to support that instrument and perform his duties under it. It is such loose doctrines that lead to arbitrary power.

He further uses the argument that this writ of habeas corpus is in the nature of an appeal, and that therefore, as far as concerns the President, it would be an assumption on the part of the judicial power to overrule his decision. Not so, Mr. President; the principle is perfectly familiar to every lawyer. The courts have decided that were a court of general jurisdiction, having jurisdiction of the particular offense, convicts the party, or commits him on proper process, it is not for them to revise and correct the irregularity of the judgment by an appeal on the writ of habeas corpus; but that is because it is the judgment of a court of justice having competent jurisdiction. Where, however, there is defect of jurisdiction, and the arrest is an excess of authority, it belongs properly to the judicial power on the writ of habeas corpus to correct the excess and guard the citizen against unlawful imprisonment. An act done in excess of authority by any department or officer is merely void, and it is a judicial question under the Constitution to determine the extent of authority. A justice of the peace has a special jurisdiction under the Constitution, and so has the President a special jurisdiction. Where ten justices of the peace committed a man on insufficient grounds, the Supreme Court, without hesitation, after sentence, as the justices had not pursued their authority, discharged the party on a return to the writ of habeas corpus. It was a conviction for non-payment of militia fines. The books are full of similar illustrations.

The learned Attorney General also contends that the writ of habeas corpus could not be directed to the President personally, where a citizen is unlawfully arrested by his order, and infers therefore that it may be disobeyed by the officer who has executed the order, and has the custody and control of the party arrested. It is a sufficient answer to say that an unlawful arrest by order of the king or privy council could always be remedied by this writ, nor could the officer executing the order refuse obedience to it.

In England he would be compelled to make return to the writ, and produce the person in his custody at the time of its service, with the cause of detention, and the court would discharge, if there was either defect of authority, or insufficient cause of detention shown. I have yet to learn that the courts of justice in the United States have less power to protect the liberty of the citizen against the arbitrary order of a President, than the King's Bench has to protect the liberty of the subject in England against unlawful arrest by the order of the monarch. There are other fallacies in this opinion which, from want of time, I forbear to notice.

Let me pass to the consideration of the dangers incident to such a claim of power in the executive, if admitted. Honorable Senators on the other side may think little of affirming this claim now; but nations, as well as individuals, are governed by habits, and habits fetter both the nation and the individual quite as effectually, and render them as helpless as Gulliver, when bound down by the little, pack threads of the Liliputians. Precedents which strike at great and fundamental principles, and violate the Constitution and the laws in times of high excitement, may be established by the party in power today. Rely upon it, if they live somewhat longer, in the progress of events, they will find that in the future they may become subject to the same dangers themselves to which now they are exposing all who are opposed to the policy and measures of this administration. The law is made, not for the protection of those who hold power, but for the protection of those who stand opposed to existing power; and no country has a Government of laws, no country is a free country, unless the law will protect them; and in that consists the distinction between a republic or a limited monarchy as a Government of laws, and a mere Government of will, which is a despotism.

Sir, I quote again from Mr. Burke:
"Parties are too apt to forget"—
    Referring to a bill for the partial suspension of the writ of habeas corpus—

"their own safety in their desire of sacrificing their enemies. People without much difficulty admit the entrance of that injustice of which they are not to be the immediate victims. In times of high proceeding, it is never the faction of the predominant power that is in danger, for no tyranny chastises its own instruments. It is the obnoxious and the suspected who want the protection of law."

The whole distinction between a government of will and a free government consists in this: That a man cannot be condemned, cannot be deprived of his personal liberty or his property, except according to the law of the land; or, in the language of Justice Curtis, without the right of contest, of being heard, and of having a judicial decision and a verdict of a jury affirming the evidence of his guilt. Sir, let me test this doctrine of suspicion in this way, and see how absurd it becomes. The Constitution of the United States, and the constitution of every State of this Union, prohibit any man from being deprived of his liberty, except by due process of law, and they secure him against conviction in criminal cases, unless on indictment and by verdict of his peers establishing his guilt. Now, sir, if he can be punished on suspicion, then to be suspected of an offense must be punishable as a crime. Is suspicion an offense against the law, or can it be made an offense? Can the suspicion of one man, however strong or however probable to him, constitute guilt which would justify, in natural right or in reason, the punishment of another? Yet you do punish when you arrest upon suspicion, because to imprison is to punish. Whether you imprison beforehand for an indefinite time by arbitrary power, or whether you imprison after a verdict of guilt, it is punishment. The difference is, that in one case the punishment is legal, as the result of crime judicially ascertained; in the other it is lawless and tyrannical, for it is founded upon the mere will of existing power.

Suppose an act were framed and passed, declaring that whenever any citizen in the State of Maryland, or, if you please, of the city of Baltimore, was found guilty of being suspected of crime by the administration, or any head of a department, on conviction thereof he should be sentenced to so many years imprisonment and so much fine: how long would the people of the United States submit to such legislation? And yet, sir, where is the difference? You would have under such a law, at least, the benefit of a verdict of a jury, and the publicity incident to a trial. The sense of shame arising from public exposure might restrain a prosecution without, at least, some plausible suspicion; but where the arrest and incarceration on suspicion is without trial, and at will, there is no liberty. If you cannot create such a crime, and punish the party after conviction, when you have ascertained judicially that he has been suspected—plausibly suspected on the part of the executive, or some of his subordinates—on what principle is it that you can punish him by imprisoning him indefinitely at the will of the President, without hearing, and without any charge against him other than suspicion, arising generally from the insinuations and whispers of personal enemies, and not unfrequently from the excited passions and distorted vision of political opponents?

Mr. President, there can be no security for personal liberty—there will be none remaining in this country—if Congress sanction, by this resolution, the President's claim of power at discretion, not only for himself, but through any of his military commanders, to suspend the great writ of habeas corpus, and take away the remedy which secures a right you cannot deny fo any citizen of the United States, that an offense against its laws shall be charged upon oath with probable cause, not of suspicion, but of guilt, and that he shall have a right to a fair and speedy trial, and only be punished upon conviction in a court of justice. Sir, I intend to make no imputation upon the motives of the President of the United States; but I must utter my disapproval of the view he takes of the Constitution, and of the mode in which he has exercised a power not delegated to him. I arraign not his intention, because I have lived long enough to know that the best men, with right intentions, have too often, from wrong judgment, perpetrated the greatest and the foulest wrong. But I take his acts—and I judge from what has passed of what will pass—when you have removed the lingering doubt that appears on the face of his message, and have affirmed that his claim of discretionary power to suspend the writ of habeas corpus is rightfully made, and that all the acts which have been done under that claim of power in the past have been rightfully done.

Merryman was arrested in the city of Baltimore—for what? For past acts, as far as we know or as was alleged. He has since been indicted for these acts—which were past acts at the time of his arrest— treason against the United States. He has been handed over to the civil power for trial, and has given bail, after having been kept in confinement by unauthorized authority for many months; and whether it was a month or three months or a week, the imprisonment was none the less an utter violation of the Constitution. But the President did not stop there. The city of Baltimore was then quiescent; the mob which existed there, (and it was a mob) was put down by the civil power of the city; order was entirely restored; and the courts of the United States have been always open. Long after, a new actor appears in the arena; and another officer of the United States, under the authority of the President, not only arrests on suspicion, without charge on oath, the chief of police of Baltimore, but without even the allegation of suspicion, he supercedes in their functions the police commissioners of that city existing under the laws of Maryland, and having the control and safeguard of its municipal protection. They were superseded without even the semblance of a suspicion charged or stated. Is such an act within the authority of the President of the United States, or of his military commanders? When these commissioners protested against this course of action, and refused to delegate to others powers entrusted to them by the legislature of Maryland solely for municipal purposes, he arrested them, too; and they are still imprisoned in Fort McHenry, without charge, without suspicion, without anything but the failure of implicit obedience to the military despot of the particular district. Not thrown into a dungeon; not manacled, that we know of; but certainly unlawfully incarcerated. The treatment, however, of these or any other prisoners confined in your forts unlawfully, must depend upon the humanity or inhumanity, the likes and dislikes, of the officer in command of the prison.

You propose to affirm all these acts by your resolution. You propose to keep these men in prison at the will of the Executive, in the face of the Constitution, for no cause stated in the proclamation of the officer who ordered the arrest having the semblance of justification. Their sole offense consisted in a refusal to delegate the powers entrusted to them by the laws of Maryland to a military commander of the United States, and yield implicit obedience to his will. Such is the course of military power always. It is an arbitrary power, and despotic in its nature. I make no particular charge against the officer who issued that order, because, I understand, he issued it under the direction of the War Department. I impugn nobody's motives; but I state the facts; and I state the facts as a gross violation of the Constitution of the United States—as an outrage upon the personal liberty of the citizen which, though it falls upon Mr. Gatchell and his associates to-day, may be brought home, gentlemen, to yourselves at a future period, if you affirm this power, because the judicial authority has been put at defiance, and the civil authority trampled upon, by military violence, and the answer is, that the writ of habeas corpus has been suspended by the President. Affirm the legality of that suspension, and of course the same answer will be given in the future; and, we all know that the military power, sustained by the Executive and by the vote of Congress, will be irresistible unless the whole people of the United States should arise *en masse* against such despotism.

Ardent as may be a man's views in favor of this war, harshly as he may think of the rebels, and determined as he may be to prosecute it to its utmost extent, until the South unconditionally submits, if he cherishes the principles of civil liberty, he cannot sustain this action of the President which violates the laws of the land, and abolishes all security for personal liberty to every citizen throughout what are called the loyal States, while it conduces, not in the slightest degree, to the subjugation or submission of the South. It touches not you now, who support and advocate the course and measures of existing power, but touches only those who are opposed to these measures; but by your approval, you take the first step for the subversion of a republican form of government, and it is the first step only which costs. The future progress toward absolutism will be rapid. Where is the necessity for the exercise of such a power, except in those States that have seceded? There I concede to you that having suspended the laws by civil war, they must take the consequences of the action of military power, if you choose to declare or recognize war. The laws of the United States are suspended in those States, and the courts are closed; but can the civil be justly and constitutionally subordinated to the military power in other States because of opposition or disaffection to the Government? Do you suppose that, by suspending the writ of habeas corpus, and authorizing the seizure of the person of an individual on suspicion, that you will ever reach the right man? You may drown all open opposition; but is the man who boldly speaks out in opposition to the measures of an administration the man who is to be feared as a conspirator?

Sir, the conspirators, if such there be, under professions of adhesion, ardent adhesion to existing power, will cloak the conspiracy by which they mean to destroy it. The slightest knowledge of human nature must lead to this conclusion. The conspirator enters into no open opposition to the Government. With the nearly unanimous support that you have, for the present at any rate, throughout all the States that have not withdrawn from the Union, you have nothing to fear, because there may be opposition to your measures, or there may be, if you please, disaffected men in all the States. Your Government is not so weak that the disaffection of a few can overturn it if supported by the people.

Look back to our own experience in history. During the revolutionary war there were Whigs and Tories, but the writ was never suspended. During Burr's conspiracy in 1807, though a single military officer arrested persons without law in New Orleans, he did not undertake to suspend the writ of habeas corpus. The Executive never approved his conduct, or claimed this power in himself. Of the three arrested, two had been sent off to the North before the writ was served; and the court in New Orleans, as to those two, held the answer sufficient that they were no longer in his custody; the third was discharged in the court there. Two were brought here, Bollman and Swartout. The President immediately handed them over to the judicial authorities with the affidavits to sustain the charge against them. The circuit court committed them for trial for treason, and on a habeas corpus before the Supreme Court, that court on revision held that the charge was not shown with sufficient certainty in the affidavits, and discharged them. Mr. Jefferson never recommended, as has been said here, that the habeas corpus law should be suspended. There is not a line or a word in his message recommending such action. He stated the fact that he had committed these men to judicial custody, and that he left to Congress to devise such measures as in their judgment they thought proper under the exigencies of the case. The Senate of the United States, in secret session—no one knows how; no one can tell what influences operated upon them, for there is no record of any debate—passed in one day, through its three readings, a bill to suspend the writ of habeas corpus; but when it came into the House of Representatives, the House of Representatives, to mark its view of the outrageous character of such an act, rejected it on its first reading, after a long debate, by a vote of 113 to 14! Yet there was a wide-spread conspiracy then, and it was in that part of the country where the Government was weakest; but no man at that day ventured to claim for the President, nor did he himself claim, the right to exercise such a power.

Then came the war of 1812. Was there no opposition or disaffection to the Government then? Was there not opposition to a very large extent during that war? Was, there not great disaffection during that war? Did the Congress of the United States suspend the writ of habeas corpus? Did the President of the United States undertake to arrest citizens and hold them in confinement at his will, claiming the right that, because war existed and communications were known to have been made to the enemy by persons disaffected to the government, therefore he might lawfully arrest any citizen on suspicion, without proof of probable cause, and detain him in prison indefinitely? No, sir, civil liberty was too much cherished in that day. Our immediate ancestors, even, knew too well what were the benefits of free government, and how insidious were the approaches and how great the curse of a despotism, to break down the Constitution under an imaginary necessity, when the Government was quite strong enough to subdue all treason, or all offenses against its laws within all the States in Which the courts were open for the prosecution of offenses, without resorting to this arbitrary exercise of power. Yet in that war we were contending against a formidable enemy, and there was serious disaffection; and the nation and the Government not half so powerful as it now is. It seems that power now too readily converts convenience into necessity.

Mr. President, human nature is the same in all ages and in all countries. Power always tends to corruption, and especially when concentrated in a single person; and it is that tendency which requires, in all free governments, the division of power among separate and independent departments, for the prevention of its abuse—legislative, executive, and judicial—and it is only by maintaining the balance between these depositories of power that a government of laws can be perpetuated. Could you suppose a god to descend upon earth for its government, it would be wiser to submit to his government than to attempt to govern ourselves; but, while humanity has its inherent frailties, the experience of mankind has vindicated the great truth that, by the concentration of power in the hands of the one or the few, a government of laws—which alone is a free government—must degenerate into a government of will. When a discretionary power over not only the property but the liberty of the citizen or subject is vested in or can be exercised by one man, uncontrolled by fundamental laws for their preservation, capable of enforcement by a separate and independent department, freedom no longer exists; and whether the person who exercises that discretionary power be called a monarch, a dictator, or a president, the government is equally a despotism. A despot may happen to have sufficient intelligence and virtue to consult the general interest of his subjects, and may govern with justice and equity, but, with the corrupting influence of power, the security is but frail for continued good government. I speak with no allusion to the present President, who may be as little affected by the possession of discretionary power as any man; but to no man, and under no emergency, should a free people ever trust uncontrolled discretionary power over their personal liberty. The power to imprison at discretion, by military force, vested in one man or a few men, is incompatible with republican institutions, be it'a dictator or a Council of Ten, the end is either despotism or oligarchy.

An honorable Senator has told us that he would be willing at this time to yield almost unlimited power to the executive. Sir if you pass this resolution, you give unlimited power to the President of the United States; you take away the last remnant of liberty in this country. You abandon to him the great judicial right which protects the liberty of the citizen, in the face of the Constitution, without judging of the exigency for yourselves, or avowing to the people, by direct legislation, that you have parted with that right. Suppose that Abraham Lincoln was a man of great force of will, of great military talent, great ambition, and with sufficient capacity as a statesman to govern and discreetly control the career of his ambition in the pursuit of permanent power. I ask you, if a Cromwell or a Bonaparte were invested with the powers you now propose to place in the hands of the President of the United States, if the liberties of this country would not lie at his feet? Sir, for one, without regard to the man, I will look upon any one in reference to the grant of such unlimited power, as a Cromwell or a Bonaparte. I cannot expect from the past history of humanity, that the next eighteen centuries will produce the equal of George Washington.

Sir, are there not dangers if this power is entrusted to the executive, apart from the idea of any attempt to obtain supreme and permanent command? Everyone knows that opposition is not readily brooked by power. We have seen that the citizen has been arrested, on mere suspicion, and without even the charge of suspicion in some cases as I have shown you. Will not the next step be to destroy the liberty of canvassing with freedom the measures of the administration; a right which is secured by our Constitution? Will not the press die under the discretionary power of arrest? If that is not sufficient, and there should be a lingering few in this chamber who venture to question any one act of the existing administration, may not the power be applied to them, and not only rebellion be crushed out in the seceded States, but the last hope of liberty crushed out, by destroying the right of the Representative of the people to boldly question the acts of power, be they those of a President, a judge, or a Congress?

Sir, I could dilate on this subject to a much greater extent; but can see that few honorable Senators opposed to me have listened to my warnings, nor will they probably have read my remarks until they pass this resolution. I suppose I must give up the faint hope I entertained, that this resolution, so utterly unnecessary to have been introduced, even on your own theory, can or will be defeated. It will pass; but, in my judgment, when you pass it, you prostrate the liberties of this country and destroy the rights of its citizens as free citizens. You must carry with you the fact that you have no condoning power, no pardoning power. You may declare an act to be legal or constitutional; but if it is not, you cannot make it so; you may legalize for the future many acts which have been done, you cannot for the past.

You cannot vest power legally by a resolution, under the Constitution, where the Constitution does not vest it. You have no judicial authority so to decree; but you may, in the face of the Constitution, by bringing the legislature into accord with the Executive in the assertion of an unconstitutional power, subvert the liberties of your country. No one has asked you—and we know we are powerless for that purpose—to censure the President of the United States; but I tell you frankly, when the people of this country pass from the state of excitement which now exists, as your resolution cannot condone any act which may have been done in violation of the Constitution by the Executive, a subsequent Congress can deal legally with this question, by the action of the House of Representatives as an impeaching body, and the action of the Senate in deciding on that impeachment. I may not then be a member of this body, and I trust I shall not. I will not attempt to predict what the action of a subsequent Congress may be on those extraordinary acts of the President which you now not only determine to approve but declare to be valid. But the very face of your resolution implies that you think they are not within his constitutional powers. By specific legislation, you may give effect to all the acts mentioned in the approving resolution, except in the case of the suspension of the writ of habeas corpus; and in regard to that, you do not venture to declare to the people of this country by open legislation the effect and object of your resolution, be it enacted by the authority of the Senate and House of Representatives, that the writ of habeas corpus shall be suspended within certain limits prescribed in the law and for a certain duration of time. Yet that is the only legitimate mode of legislation when the necessity arises, and the only constitutional mode in which such a power can be exercised.

About James A. Bayard

James A. Bayard (1799-1880) was a United States
Senator from Delaware. His father, James A. Bayard,
cast the deciding vote in the 1800 presidential election,
and his grandfather, Richard Bassett, signed the
Constitution. His brother, son, and grandson also served
in the United States Senate. Bayard was one of the lone
voices of opposition to the Lincoln administration during
the War.

Additional Resources

Holey Union: The Constitutional Paradox of Secession, by Rivka Weil [83]

"Studying the delicate dance of constitutional democracies and secessionist movements not only enables a better understanding of constitutional law but may also shed new scholarly light on assumptions that Constitutions are generally silent about secession and may even implicitly allow it."

Recognition and Secessionist in the Complex Environment of World Politics, by Steven Michael Wheatly [84]

"The focus of this paper is the external aspect of the right: the right to Statehood and secession."

Secession's theory (Remedial Right Only Theories), by Aziz Sheikhani [85]

"This article investigates the right of people to secede from their rulers. The ending of the Cold War gave more chances for the emergence of new states."

Splitsylvania: State Secession and What to Do About It, by Glenn Harlan Reynolds [86]

"This short piece looks at the growing phenomenon of intra-state secession movements." The author is of the opinion that there are other ways to resolve deficient between the needs of minority and disaffected groups and existing constitutional arrangements.

On the Right to External Self-Determination: 'Selfistans,' Secession and the Great Powers' Rule, by Milena Sterio [87]

"*This Article will posit that the right to external self-determination accrues for different peoples if and when the Great Powers decide to recognize those peoples' causes. Ultimately, this Article will argue that such a result is unfortunate, as it inappropriately mixes the legal with the political realms, and that any rule by the Great Powers inherently challenges the notion of state sovereignty and equality.*" Sterio's observation is a pragmatic one, well known in history. The great democratic nations espouse the concepts of self-determination but in practical application, secession and devolution movements have only been accepted, supported and legitimized when those movements fall within the interest of the great powers.

Bibliography

[1] Jon Henley, Finbarr Sheehy , Glenn Swann and Chris Fenn. "Beyond Catalonia: pro-independence movements in Europe". https://www.theguardian.com/world/ng-interactive/2017/oct/27/beyond-catalonia-pro-independence-movements-in-europe-map

[2] (Emerson 1967) p. 450

[3] (Calhoun 1831)

[4] (Articles of Confederation : March 1, 1781)

[5] (J. Buchanan 1860)

[6] (Birch 1984)

[7] (Wells 1920)

[8] (Calhoun 1831)

[9] (Ferrari 2000)

[10] (Cooke 1961), (Berger 1987)

[11] (Definitive Treaty of Peace 1783)

[12] (Ratification of the Constitution by the State of Virginia; June 26, 1788)

[13] (Kaminski 1993)

[14] (The Articles of Confederation of the United Colonies of New England; May 19, 1643)

[15] (Articles of Confederation : March 1, 1781)

[16] (Gannon n.d.), (Amendments to the Constitution Proposed by the Hartford Convention : 1814)

[17] (Definitive Treaty of Peace 1783)

[18] (Constitution of Vermont - July 8, 1777)

[19] (Articles of Confederation : March 1, 1781)

[20] (B. L. Clark 2016)

[21] (Declaration of Independence, July 4, 1776)

[22] (Taylor 2003)

[23] (Suthon 1953)

[24] (McElwee 1958)

[25] (Unconstitutional Creation of the Fourteenth 1960)

[26] (Call 1961) (The Fourteenth Amendment and Its Skeptical Background 1963), (Fernandez 1966)

[27] (Avins 1967)

[28] (J. B. James, The Framing of the Fourteenth Amendment 1956)

[29] (J. B. James 1984)

[30] (Congressional Globe 1866)

[31] (Historical Statistics of the United States) p. 693
[32] (Congressional Globe 1866) p. 3042
[33] (Debates and Proceedings of the Congress of the United States 1789) p. 766
[34] (Debates and Proceedings 646-684 (6-7 December 1803) 1920) the Supreme Court confirmed this interpretation, ruling that two-thirds of a quorum is adequate.
[35] (Kelly 1970) p. 455
[36] (Flack 1965) p. 140. (J. B. James 1984) pp. 5-7
[37] (J. B. James 1984) pp. 11-24
[38] Ibid. pp. 56-58
[39] Ibid. pp. 79-95
[40] Ibid. pp. 97-99, 105-107, 109-112, 118-119, 227, 277
[41] Ibid. pp. 123-131, 152-154, 157-158, 168-169
[42] (Richardson 1898) p. 434. Texas v. White, 7 Wallace 700 (1869); White v. Hart, 80 U.S. 646 (1871); *Luther v. Borden*, 7 Howard 1 (1849). GEORGIA JOURNAL OF SOUTHERN LEGAL HISTORY
[43] (Richardson 1898) pp. 282-288, 300. The relevant cases are *Fairchild v. Hughes*, 258 U.S. 126 (1922) and Coleman v. Miller, 307 U.S. 433 (1939). The latter discusses the Fourteenth Amendment and says that the decision by the "political departments of the government as to the validity of the adoption of the Fourteenth Amendment has been accepted." Certain aspects of the process, however, have been held to be justiciable. *Hollingsworth v. Virginia*, 3 Dallas 378 (1798); *Hawke v. Smith*, 253 U.S. 231 (1920); Dillon v. Gloss, 256 U.S. 368 (1921).
[44] On this subject of radicals and nonradicals, the definitive work is Michael Les Benedict, Congressional Republicans and Reconstruction, 18631869 (1974).
[45] Statutes at Large 428, 15:12, 14
[46] (Suthon 1953) p. 30. The new constitutions and Mississippi's amendments are in Francis Newton Thorpe, The Federal and State Constitutions 1:116, 288, 2:685, 809, 3:1429, 4:2066, 5:2799, 6:3269, 3569, 7:3852 (1909).
[47] (McElwee 1958) pp. 492-500.

[48] (Congressional Globe 1866) 2d Session, Part 3, 1,644

[49] Mississippi v. Johnson, 4 Wallace 475 (1867); Georgia v. Stanton, 6 Wallace 50 (1867).

[50] Wallace 506 (1869). For a thorough account of the McCardle case, see 2 Charles Warren, The Supreme Court in United States History (1922) pp. 465, 473-488. See also Stanley Kutler, "*Ex Parte* McCardle: Judicial Impotency? The Supreme Court and Reconstruction Reconsidered 72 American Historical Review (1967).

[51] Congressional Globe, 40th Congress, 2d Session, 1417 (25 February 1868).

[52] (J. B. James 1984) pp. 233-239

[53] (B. L. Clark 2016) p.2

[54] (Burke 2002) pp. 557-559

[55] Ibid. pp. 556-557

[56] (Hines 2012) pp. 97-98

[57] (Woods)

[58] (Lawrence 1957)

[59] (McDonald 1982)

[60] (Calvin)

[61] This was in reference to the impeding American Revolution, a secession of the American colonies from Britain.

[62] (Stampp 1980) pp. 35-36

[63] (Tilley 1991) p. 248

[64] (The Right of Secession, The New-York Daily Tribune December 17, 1860 1964) pp. 199-201

[65] Ibid. "We have repeatedly asked those who dissent from our view of this matter to tell us frankly whether they do or do not assent to Mr. Jefferson's statement in the Declaration of Independence that governments "derive their just powers from the consent of the governed; and that, whenever any form of government becomes destructive of these ends, it is the right of the people to alter or abolish it, and to institute a new government," &c., &c. We do heartily accept this doctrine, believing it intrinsically sound, beneficent, and one that, universally accepted, is calculated to prevent the shedding of seas of human blood. And, if it justified the secession from the British Empire of Three Millions of colonists in 1776, we do not see why it would not justify the secession of Five Millions of Southrons from the Federal Union in 1861. If we are mistaken on this point, why does not some one attempt to show wherein and why? . . . --we could

[66] (Madison 1840) p.895

[67] (Morse 1986) pp. 422-427

[68] (Chicago-Kent College of Law at Illinois Tech 1824)

[69] (Morse 1986) pp. 428-432

[70] (Benjamin 1907)

[71] (Morse 1986) p.433

[72] Ibid. pp. 433-434

[73] Ibid. pp. 434-436

[74] Ibid. 436

[75] (The Southern Essays of Richard M. Weaver 1987)

[76] (Bledsoe 1866)

[77] (The Southern Essays of Richard M. Weaver 1987) p. 152

[78] Taking on Webster also challenges most of the others who did not believe the Constitution was a compact, because most of the others quoted Webster and used his argument.

[79] (Bledsoe 1866) p. 6

[80] (Tocqueville 1831) p. 413

[81] (B. I. Clark 2012)

[82] "The Calhoun Review, Issue 1, Volume I, 2016 – Secession and Devolution in Contemporary Geopolitical Theory" (2016) Available at:
http://www.calhouninstitute.com/review/Calhoun_Review_Vol1_no1_2016.pdf

[83] Weill, Rivka, Holey Union: The Constitutional Paradox of Secession (November 27, 2014). Available at SSRN:http://ssrn.com/abstract=2708859 or http://dx.doi.org/10.2139/ssrn.2708859

[84] Wheatley, Steven Michael. "Recognition and secession in the complex environment of world politics." (2015): 135-144. http://eprints.lancs.ac.uk/78211/2/Fribourg_Paper_FIN_2014_09_29.pdf

 [85] Sheikhani, Aziz. "Secession's theory (Remedial Right Only Theories)."Journal of Advances in Political Science 2, no. 3. http://citeseerx.ist.psu.edu/viewdoc/download?doi=10.1.1.671.2583&rep=rep1&type=pdf

[86] Reynolds, Glenn Harlan, Splitsylvania: State Secession and What to Do About It (March 1, 2018). University of Tennessee Legal Studies Research Paper No. 343. Available at SSRN: https://ssrn.com/abstract=3130497 or http://dx.doi.org/10.2139/ssrn.3130497

[87] Sterio, Milena, On the Right to External Self-Determination: 'Selfistans,' Secession and the Great Powers' Rule (April 23, 2009). Minnesota Journal of International Law, Vol. 19, 2010; Cleveland-Marshall Legal Studies Paper No. 09-163. Available at SSRN: https://ssrn.com/abstract=1337172

Adams, Charles. 2000. When in the Course of Human Events: Arguing the Case for Southern Secession. Lanham: Rowman and Littlefield.

Amendments to the Constitution Proposed by the Hartford Convention : 1814. The Avalon Project. http://avalon.law.yale.edu/19th_century/hartconv.asp

Articles of Confederation : March 1, 1781. The Avalon Project. Articles of Confederation : March 1, 1781.

Avins, Alfred. 1967. The Reconstruction Amendments' Debates. Virginia Commission on Constitutional Government. https://books.google.com/books?id=isKFAAAAMAAJ

Benjamin, Judah P. 1907. Farewell Address to the U.S. Senate, February 5, 1861. Vol. 1, in Library of Southern Literature, edited by Joel Chandler Harris Edwin Anderson Alderman. Atlanta: The Martin Holt Company. https://books.google.com/books?id=RcmPQtF-mXcC .

Berger, Raoul. 1987. Federalism: The Founder's Design. Norman: University of Oklahoma Press.

Birch, Anthony H. 1984. "Another Liberal Theory of Secession." POLITICAL STUDIES 32 (4): 596 - 602. doi:10.1111/j.1467-9248.1984.tb01548.x.

Bledsoe, Albert Taylor. 1866. Is Davis a traitor; or, Was secession a constitutional right previous to the war of 1861? Baltimore: Innes & Company. https://books.google.com/books?id=S28FAAAAQAAJ.

Buchanan, Allen. 1991. Secession. Bolder: Westview Press.

Buchanan, James. 1860. Fourth Annual Message to Congress on the State of the Union. http://www.presidency.ucsb.edu/ws/?pid=29501.

Burke. 2002. "Unorthodox and Paradox: Revisiting the Ratification of the Fourteenth Amendment." Alabama Law Review 53:2 (555). http://www.law.ua.edu/pubs/lrarticles/Volume%2053/Issue%202/Bryant .pdf.

Calhoun, John C. 1831. "A Discourse on the Constitution and Government of the United States." In Union and Liberty: The Political Philosophy of John C. Calhoun, edited by Ross M. Lence. Indianapolis: Liberty Fund.

Call, Joseph L. 1961. "The Fourteenth Amendment Amendment." Baylor Law Review. Calvin, John. n.d. Institutes of the Christian Religion. Vol. IV. https://books.google.com/books?id=zT5lCwAAQBAJ.

Cheek, H. Lee. 2001. Calhoun and Popular Rule. Columbia: University Jof Missouri Press.

Chicago-Kent College of Law at Illinois Tech. 1824. Gibbons v. Ogden.
https://www.oyez.org/cases/1789-1850/22us1.

Clark, Barry lee. 2012. "Manifesto of Old Men and Simple Preachers." Social Science
Research Network- Political Philosophy eJournal. http://ssrn.com/abstract=2732840.

Clark, Barry Lee. 2016. "The First War of the New Order: How Rule of Law and the Form of Government Changed in America's Second Revolution." SSRN. doi:10.13140/RG.2.1.5163.7528.
http://ssrn.com/abstract=2728971

1866. "Congressional Globe." 39th Congress. Constitution of Vermont - July 8, 1777. The Avalon Project.
http://avalon.law.yale.edu/18th_century/vt01.asp.

Cooke, Jacobs E., ed. 1961. The Federalist. (Middletown, Conn.: Wesleyan University Press.

Curry, Jabaz L. 1895. The Southern States of the American Union Considered in their Relations to the Constitution of the United States and the Resulting Union. Richmond: R.F. Johnston Publishing.
https://books.google.com/books?id=QCQUAAAAYAAJ.

Dabney, Robert L. 1867. "A Defence of Virfinia and Through Her of the South." New York: E.J. Hale and Son.
https://books.google.com/books?id=PwVnt4hozogC.

Davis, Jefferson. 1881. "The Rise and Fall of the Confederate Government."
https://books.google.com/books?id=nazZyJc1J3sC.

1920. "Debates and Proceedings 646-684 (6-7 December 1803)." In National Prohibition Cases, 253 U.S.

1789. "Debates and Proceedings of the Congress of the United States."
n.d. "Declaration of Independence, July 4, 1776." (The Avalon Project).

http://avalon.law.yale.edu/18th_century/declare.asp.

n.d. "Definitive Treaty of Peace 1783." Library of Congress. Accessed FEB 5, 2016. https://memory.loc.gov/cgibin/ampage?collId=llsl&fileName=008/llsl008.db&recNum=93.

Emerson, Rupert. 1967. From Empire to Nation. Cambridge: Harvard University. https://books.google.com/books/about/From_empire_to_nation.html?id=H8A1AAAAIAAJ.

Fernandez, Ferdinand F. 1966. "The Constitutionality of the Fourteenth Amendment." Southern California Law Review 39.

Ferrari, G. R. F., Griffith, Tom. 2000. Plato The Republic. Cambridge University Press. https://books.google.com/books?id=aPwPjVIxbGQC.

Flack, Horace Edgar. 1965. The Adoption of the Fourteenth Amendment.
Freehling, William W. 1990. The Road to Disunion: Secessionist at Bay, 1776-1854. New York: Oxford University Press.

Gannon, Kevin. Nullification, Secession, or a "Great Pamphlet?": New England Federalism and the Hartford Convention Movement, 1809-1815. https://www.academia.edu/9598540/Nullification_Secession_or_a_Great_Pamphlet_New_England_Federalism_and_the_Hartford_Convention_Movement_1809-1815.

Gildersleeve, Basil L. 1915. "The Creed of the Old South." Baltimore: The Johns Hopkins Press. https://books.google.com/books?id=ISh3AAAAMAAJ.

Gordon, David, ed. 1998. Seccesion, State and Liberty. New Brunswick: Transaction Publishers.

Hines, Eric. 2012. A Conservative's Treatise on American Government. Xlibris Corporation. https://books.google.com/books?id=dLB1v4Smbz4C.

"Historical Statistics of the United States."

James, Joseph B. 1956. The Framing of the Fourteenth Amendment. University of Illinois Press.
https://books.google.com/books?id=yI6BXwAACAAJ.

James, Joseph Bliss. 1984. The Ratification of the Fourteenth Amendment. Mercer University Press.
https://books.google.com/books?id=vZGbAAAAMAAJ.

Kaminski, John P., Saladino, Gaspare J. et al., ed. 1993. The Documentary History of the Raification of the Constitution, Volumes VIII-X: Ratification of the Constitution by the States, Virginia. Madison: State Historical Society of Wisconson.

Kelly, Alfred H. 1970. The American Constitution: Its Origins and Development. 4th.

Lawrence, David. 1957. "There is no Fourteenth Amendment." U.S. News and World Report. Accessed Feb 5, 2016.
http://www.constitution.org/14ll/no14th.htm.

Madison, James. 1840. The Madison Papers.
https://books.google.com/books?id=UMLKZwEACAAJ.

McDonald, Forrest. 1982. A Constitutional History of the United States. R.E. Krieger
Publishing Company.
https://books.google.com/books?id=CJIYAAAAYAAJ.

McElwee, Pinckney G. 1958. "The 14th Amendment to the Constitution of the United States and the Threat That It Poses to Our Democratic." South Carolina Law Quarterly 11.

Morris, Gouverneur. 1832. Life and Writings. Vol. III.
https://books.google.com/books?id=IfluUp9fEeYC.

Morse, Newcomb. 1986. "The Foundations and Meaning of Secession." Stetson Law Review (Stetson University College of Law) XV (2): 419-436.
http://www.worldcat.org/title/foundations-and-meaning-of-secession/oclc/855706851.

Pollard, Edward A. 1867. The Lost Cause. Baltimore: E.B.
Treat and Company.
https://books.google.com/books?id=v2wFAAAAQAAJ.

Ratification of the Constitution by the State of Virginia;
June 26, 1788. The Avalon Project.
http://avalon.law.yale.edu/18th_century/ratva.asp.

Review, Calhoun. Barry Clark. "The Calhoun Review,
Issue 1, Volume I, 2016 – Secession and Devolution in
Contemporary Geopolitical Theory" (2016)
Available at:
http://www.calhouninstitute.com/review/Calhoun_Review_Vol1_no1_2016
.pdf

Rawle, William. 1829. A view of the Constitution of the
United States of America. P.H. Nicklin.
https://books.google.com/books?id=PicTAAAAYAAJ.

Richardson, James D. 1898. A Compilation of the
Messages and Papers of the Presidents, 1789-1897.

Smith, Goldwyn. 1893. The United States: an Outline of
Political History, 1492-1871.
New York and London.
https://books.google.com/books?id=nxUTAAAAYAAJ.

Stampp, Kennith M. 1980. The Imperiled Union, Essays
on the Background of the Civil War. New York: Oxdord
University Press.
https://books.google.com/books?id=ZGWTbIew8ekC.

Stephens, Alexander H. "A Constitutional View of the
Late War Between the States."
https://books.google.com/books?id=GZwqlWCQhr0C.

Suthon, Walter J. Jr. 1953. "The Dubious Origin of the
Fourteenth Amendment." Tulane Law Review 28.

Taylor, Michael J. C. 2003. "A More Perfect Union':
Ableman v. Booth and the Culmination of Federal
Sovereignty." Journal of Supreme Court History 28 (2).
doi:10.1111/1540-5818.00058.

n.d. The Articles of Confederation of the United Colonies of New England; May 19, 1643. The Avalon Project. http://avalon.law.yale.edu/17th_century/art1613.asp.

1963. "The Fourteenth Amendment and Its Skeptical Background." Alabama Law Review.

1964. "The Right of Secession, The New-York Daily Tribune December 17, 1860." In Northern Editorials on Secession, edited by Howard Cecil Perkins. Gloucester: Peter Smith. https://books.google.com/books?id=gdomcgAACAAJ.

1987. "The Southern Essays of Richard M. Weaver." In The Southern Essays of Richard M. Weaver, edited by James J. Thompson Jr. George M. Curtis III. Indianapolis: Liberty Press. https://books.google.com/books?id=hwUSAAAAYAAJ.

Tilley, John Shipley. 1991. "Abraham Lincoln, 1847, Congressional Debate in the United States House of Representatives." In Lincoln Takes Command. Nashville: Bill Coats, Ltd. https://books.google.com/books?id=L013AAAAMAAJ

Tocqueville, Alexis de. 1831. Democracy in America.
Page | 108
https://books.google.com/books?id=UXkJ0gvjSOAC.

1960. "Unconstitutional Creation of the Fourteenth." Georgia Bar Journal.

Wells, H.G. 1920. The Outline of History. New York: P.F. Colier and Son Company. https://books.google.com/books?id=uCcQAAAAYAAJ.

Woods, Thomas E. Jr. n.d. The 14th Amendment Never Ratified. Accessed Feb 5, 2016. https://www.youtube.com/watch?v=nMfkACt0yLw